The Homemade Year

Lilly Higgins is a TV chef, food and wine writer, and food photographer. She writes a weekly recipe column for the *Irish Times* and appears regularly on RTÉ television's afternoon programme, *The Today Show*. She won an award for her cookery writing at the 2021 Irish Food Writing Awards. Lilly has a BA in Design from Cork Institute of Technology and completed the 12-week Ballymaloe Cookery Certificate. She has previously published two cookbooks with Gill Books: *Make, Bake, Love* and *Dream Deli*. Lilly loves nothing more than pottering around the house creating a cosy, comfortable nest for herself and her family. In this, her third book (which she photographed and styled herself), she shares an inspirational collection of ideas for things to make, do and enjoy in the home. Lilly lives in Cobh with her husband and three children.

The Homemade Year

Things to make, do and eat at home to welcome every season

Lilly Higgins

Gill Books

Gill Books
Hume Avenue
Park West
Dublin 12
www.gillbooks.ie

Gill Books is an imprint of M.H. Gill and Co.

9780717193806

Designed by www.grahamthew.com
Print origination by Bartek Janczak
Edited by Esther Ní Dhonnacha
Proofread by Jane Rogers
Printed and bound by Printer Trento, Italy
This book is typeset in 8.5/11pt, Sofia Pro

*The paper used in this book comes from the wood
pulp of sustainably managed forests.*

A CIP catalogue record for this book is available
from the British Library.

5 4 3 2 1

Acknowledgements

Thanks so much to the amazing team at Gill for working on this book with me. It all started as an idea eight years ago with Nicki Howard; we planned a nostalgic crafting book and now it's come to life with a modern twist. We finally have this gorgeous book to be proud of. Thanks to the brilliant Teresa Daly for believing in me and being such a wonderful support. I couldn't have done this without you.

Thanks to Graham Thew for the beautiful design. This is our third book together and you managed to create the exact look I wanted, even though it's so fresh and different from the others. Thank you!

Much appreciation to Rachel Thompson, Rachael Kilduff and Aoibheann Molumby for editing, crossing my t's and dotting my i's; and to Laura King and Bartek Janczak for their meticulous work on the layout.

Thanks to the very talented Gillian Carney for taking the photos of me. I always wanted to work with you on this book and am so lucky to have you as a friend.

Huge thanks as ever to my amazing parents and siblings – especially to Rosie, my right-hand woman.

Gratitude to Colm for his never-ending love and support of my work and all that I do. Teamwork makes the dream work!

Liam, Cathal and Hazel: my sun, moon and stars. Thanks for inspiring me every day to be creative in all that ye do. Ye're amazing little legends and I adore ye xxx

Contents

Introduction

This is a creative handbook to guide you joyfully through the year, using seasonal crafts and projects to renew your sense of wonder and connectivity to the natural world. Thinking back, it's a book I've been writing my whole life. My parents always taught us to go where our hearts lead us and follow our dreams. So, after secondary school, I ping-ponged from course to course: I spent a year studying art, another year studying animation and four years earning my bachelor's degree in design. Once I completed those six years of intense creativity, I packed my bags and enrolled in Ballymaloe Cookery School. Art and food are always so connected: both involve creating and I love that. I was soaking up different skills but unsure of how to use them.

This book is a combination of all that learning, a way for creativity to seep into our everyday lives, bringing joy in small, rewarding projects that are fun to do and get great results. All of these crafts are centred on sustainability – you won't find a pipe cleaner in this book! But with a basic arsenal of paper, glue, twine and sticky tape, you can create magic. And creativity can often be a spur-of-the-moment thing; when a window of time suddenly opens up (the baby is sleeping or that Zoom call is cancelled!), having to run to the shop for special equipment can dampen the mood.

There are at least six projects for each month, ranging from seasonal celebrations or self-care to kid-friendly activities and tasty recipes, and all are guided by the Irish calendar year. These projects are about making the most of what we've got, providing inspiration for creativity off-screen, slowing down and making the everyday moments special. As we've all discovered, it's more important than ever to celebrate the small things.

Spring
Imbolc

February, March, April

Spring has sprung! The bird is on the wing. Why, that's absurd! I always thought the wing was on the bird!

There are so many versions of the little poem above. It's quite impossible to track down its origins. My maternal grandfather taught it to us when we were little. He loved poetry and stories, writing something pretty much every day himself. He loved seeing spring unfold. This season is all about waking from hibernation, birds returning, opening our eyes and embracing nature once more as those green shoots appear. Stretching like cats after a long sleep. There are so many simple ways you can embrace and celebrate the joy of this season through crafts, nature and seasonal recipes which I will suggest in this section.

We kick off the season with Imbolc, the first two days of February, the first days of spring. It's midway through the dark half of the year and it celebrates both the pagan goddess Bríde and the Catholic Saint Brigid. Candlemas falls on 2 February and there are many sayings around weather and predictive superstitions surrounding this day. It's the day animals are traditionally said to leave hibernation (the North American tradition Groundhog Day, and the movie of the same name, are about exactly this moment!).

Imbolc is all about acknowledging the return of growth and the regeneration of spring. It's a month for sowing vegetables and generally tidying up the garden. It's something I always feel like doing at this time of year anyway, discovering how my herb bed has survived the winter and checking on spring bulbs. Getting outside and clearing away leaves, making room for new growth to emerge.

Imbolc is followed closely by Valentine's Day and then St Patrick's Day in March. In late March or April comes Easter with pretty pastel colours, more flowers emerging and so much chocolate! Our calendar of events fills up fast. There are so many changes to notice in nature and so much to appreciate as this new fresh season begins.

Over the years Valentine's Day has morphed into a general appreciation and declaration of love for those you cherish. Telling your friends and family how much you adore them as well as showering affection on your one true love, of course. It's more of a gratitude-fest and an annual reminder that we should be telling those we love that we love them more often.

It's great to start this new season with an appreciation of nature and those around us. The enjoyable projects I suggest in the following pages help us to do just that. Celebrate new life with Imbolc and make a St Brigid's Day cross, then settle down to making your own cards, envelopes and delicious chocolate treats for your loved ones on Valentine's Day. Next, dust off the cobwebs and spring clean your house with a beautiful infused vinegar. The festivities continue with St Patrick's Day and there are plenty of ways to decorate your home with woven placemats and rosettes. We roll into April looking forward to family gatherings, an Easter egg hunt and a rainbow of multicoloured eggs. I hope you find so much joy in these projects celebrating spring, one of the most life-affirming seasons of them all.

A St Brigid's Day cross

What you'll need:

Paper
Sellotape
Scissors

1 February is Imbolc, the pagan holiday based on Celtic tradition. It marks the halfway point between the winter solstice and the spring equinox. Like all pre-Christian celebrations, it highlights an aspect of sunlight and heralds the change of seasons. It feels good to tap into these pagan traditions because, I think, it feels natural. Reading the seasons around us and feeling, quite literally, the winds of change makes perfect sense. These celebrations usually involve the flowers that are growing at that moment and the bounty that nature provides. Creating a cross from rushes or straw for St Brigid's Day is the perfect example. These would traditionally have been placed in every home and outbuilding until the following February to bless them. Almost everyone would make one, and those who could not would be gifted one. If you can't source rushes, then use scraps of paper for a pretty and simple craft to decorate your home.

Method

1 Decorate your paper however you like; each cross is unique to you and your family. Drawing, colouring or using watercolours can all look lovely!
2 Cut the paper into four equal-sized strips – my strips were 29cm long and 4cm wide. You can use any size you like; this is just a guide.
3 Fold the strips in half and assemble them as in these photos.
4 Once assembled, slot all pieces tightly together and use a piece of Sellotape at the back to secure them in place.

Lilly's tips

▶ Why not try using pages from a pretty book or spare bits of wrapping paper to make your strips?

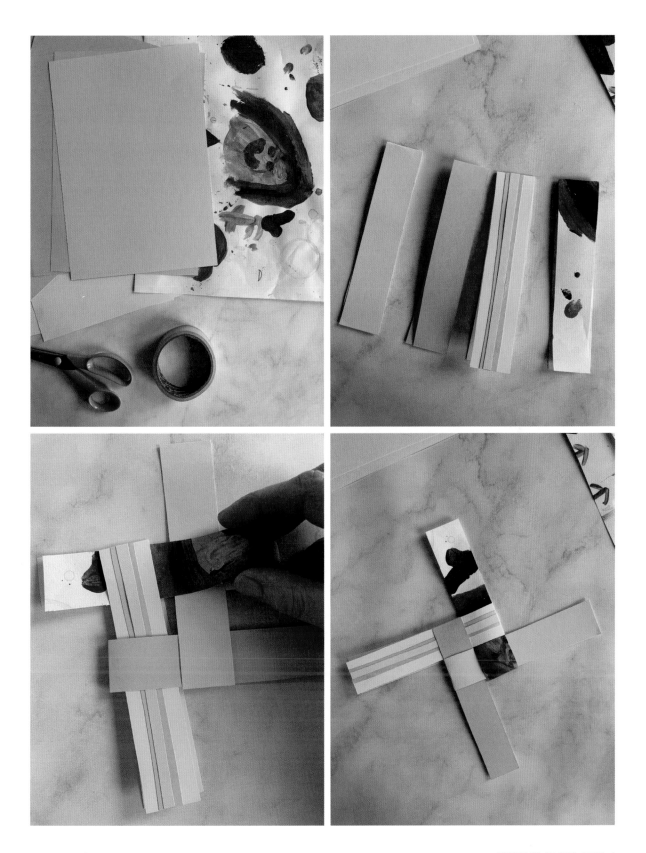

DIY envelope

What you'll need:

1 square of paper, a little larger than the card you want to enclose
Sellotape or glue stick

This craft is so handy to know! So many times we've made cards or drawings and I can't find an envelope that fits. This technique enables you to make a snug-fitting envelope of any size. All you need is a square of paper slightly larger than your card. I tend to use brown paper bags for these, especially if I need a larger one. Just disassemble the brown paper bag and remove any handles, then iron the paper flat between two towels. You can then store it and use it for projects like this.

Here are sample sizes for cards to give an example of square size:
For an A5 card use a 30cm x 30cm square.
For a 10cm x 12.5cm card use an 18cm x 18cm square.

Method

1 Turn the square of paper into a diamond shape so that its corners are left and right, top and bottom.
2 Centre your card in the middle of the diamond. Fold each corner over your card.
3 Unfold the square and remove the card. Cut away the triangles where the fold lines cross.
4 Now fold the sides in and fold the bottom flap over them.
5 Cut the point off the bottom flap and glue the edges of the bottom flap to the lower edges of the side flaps.
6 To finish, put your card inside and glue the top down, or seal closed with a piece of tape and a wax seal (see page 14).

Homemade wax seal

What you'll need:

A coloured crayon – red is great and
   so vibrant
Scrap paper
A candle
An old tablespoon
An embossed button or coin with a
   raised pattern to use as a seal
Pritt Stick
An envelope or paper

There's something very 'Another letter from Mr Darcy has just arrived, Ma'am' about wax seals, isn't there? I can imagine his furrowed brow and tousled curls as he stamps his signet ring into the warm wax. Swoon!

I first came across wax seals in my granddad's study. He had an amazing typewriter that we loved to write letters on and an endless supply of white A4 sheets. He had a stamp and sealing wax for envelopes, a stapler and lots of ink pots with fountain pens. We loved to just mooch around his study, opening drawers and generally being nosy. He was a prolific reader and had stacks of books absolutely everywhere. We would usually come across toffees too. He loved sweets so always had a stash hidden somewhere!

This wax seal looks so pretty and finishes off an envelope so beautifully. Details of how to make your own envelope are on page 12. Keep in mind this wax seal should only be used for hand-delivered letters and is quite delicate. You can buy sealing wax online or in craft stores, though, to make an authentic seal.

Caution: Please be careful with hot wax and flames as both can burn.

Method

1 Peel the wrapper away from your crayon. Break the crayon into small pieces.
2 Practise first on a piece of scrap paper. Rub the glue wherever you are planning on putting the wax seal; this is to strengthen it.
3 Light the candle and place a few pieces of crayon on the spoon.
4 Place the spoon over the flame till the wax has melted.
5 Once the wax has melted leave it to cool for 20 seconds before making a little puddle from the wax on your glued spot. The puddle should be a little larger than the button or coin you have.
6 Leave the wax for a few seconds to cool a little, then press the button or coin into the wax. Leave it there for 30 seconds till the wax cools a little more, then carefully remove the button or coin. Ta-da!
7 Now that you've practised, repeat these steps with your envelope.

Lilly's tips

▶ Use a drizzle of wax to glue a dried flower sprig or eucalyptus twig on a package or envelope. No need to stamp, just pour it on and press the flower sprig or twig into the wax.

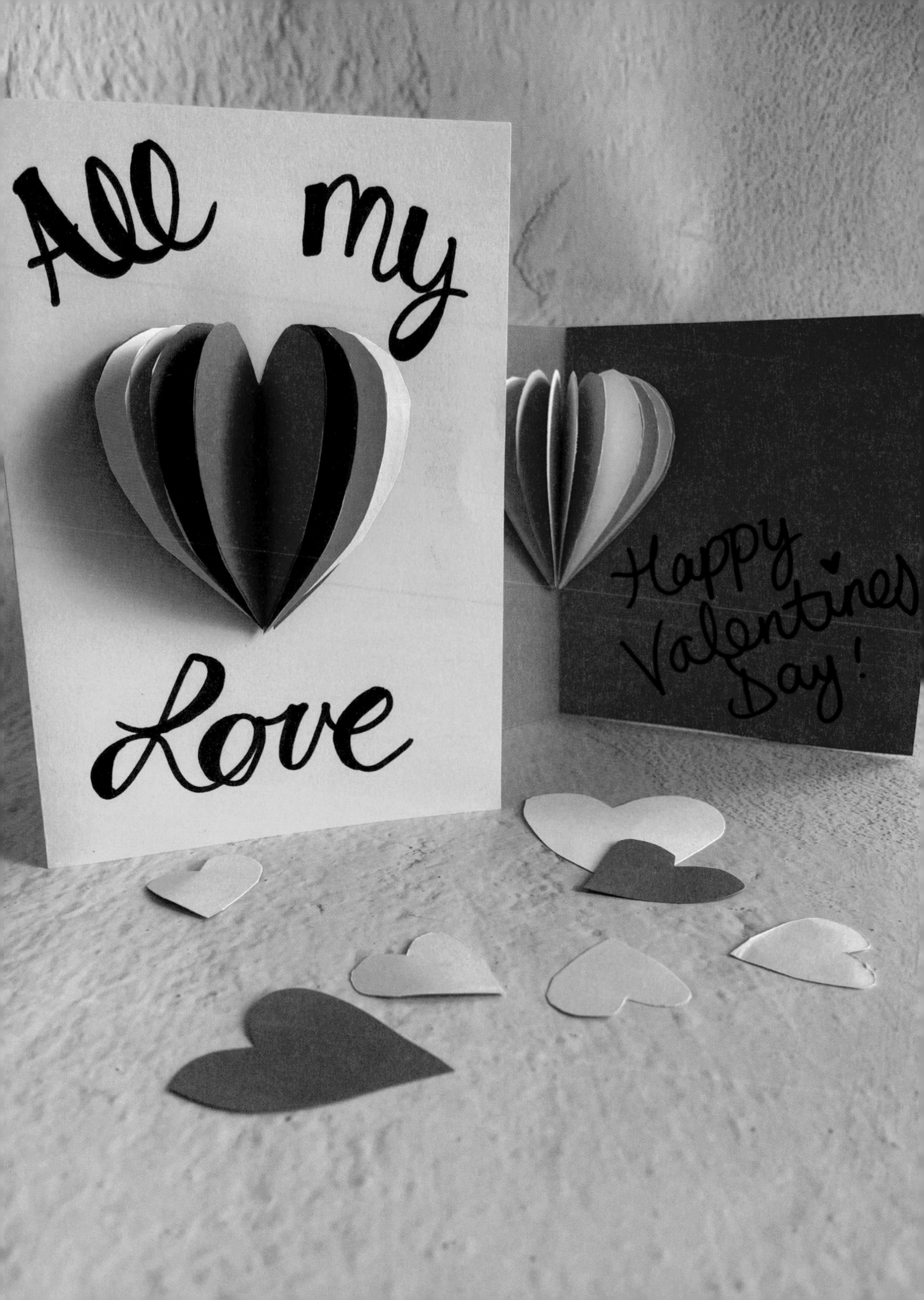
All my
Love
Happy Valentines Day!

Valentine's Day card

What you'll need:

1 A4 piece of heavy paper stock or card
Different-coloured paper or card
Pritt Stick or other glue
Scissors
Pencil

14 February is Valentine's Day. I love Valentine's cards that have that extra wow factor. This one is very easy to make and is so unique. You can use card, paper or even photos of your loved ones to make the heart shapes. Do a series of 3D hearts or just one in the centre. The heart is great on the outside or makes a great surprise on the inside.

My parents have kept so many of the cards and drawings we made for them when we were little. We used to love going through the big chest of them. It's like a make-and-do time capsule with drawings, knitted mementos and paintings all done by their eight children – and now some of the grandchildren's artwork is in there too. We have a similar box for our children and already they love looking through their cotton wool snowman pictures and the handprints from their first days of playschool. I'm like a magpie and find it hard to part with their beautiful drawings.

It's so much fun to make your own cards for different occasions and this simple design will work for so many of life's celebrations.

Method

1 Fold one piece of heavy card in half to make the card.
2 Draw out a heart shape on one of your coloured sheets and make nine more exact copies of it in different colours.
3 Glue one heart to the centre of the card.
4 Fold the nine other hearts evenly in half.
5 Glue the central 'spine' of one of the folded heart halves onto the flat heart. Then glue another half onto that. Continue adding glue and adding folded paper hearts until your 3D heart is complete.

Truffles

What you'll need:

140g dark chocolate
60g milk chocolate
25g salted butter
150ml cream
Toppings: cocoa, toasted coconut, finely chopped hazelnuts, freeze-dried raspberries, finely chopped pistachios

Makes 12

For Valentine's Day it's just got to be chocolate. There really is nothing like homemade chocolate truffles. We've been making these for years and there are so many different variations. Add a pinch of chilli powder, orange zest or powdered ginger, or finely chopped candied ginger. Use Irish cream liqueur instead of cream at Christmas for a delicious truffle that's amazing with coffee.

The key here is to place the truffle mix in the fridge for long enough. I sometimes even pop it in the freezer for a while to firm up. It does get a little messy, so have everything prepared first. Make sure to wash your hands regularly to avoid getting chocolate everywhere. Place all the coatings in separate little bowls, ready to roll. You can make tiny truffles and roll them in sprinkles for birthday parties.

My favourite way to have these is to place one toasted hazelnut inside and roll the truffle in finely chopped toasted hazelnuts. It's the most delicious homemade Ferrero Rocher that everyone is sure to love. With these homemade truffles I am really spoiling you!

Method

1 Chop up the chocolate and place in a heatproof bowl over a pan of simmering water.
2 Once the chocolate is almost melted, add the butter and stir to combine. Remove the pan from the heat. Add the cream and stir quickly to combine. The mixture will look split, but just keep stirring and it will get thicker and creamier. Transfer to another bowl to help cool it faster, then place in the fridge for at least 3 hours.
3 Line a tray with greaseproof paper.
4 Prepare all your coatings and put them in separate bowls or saucers. Scoop a tablespoon of the chocolate truffle mix and roll it gently in the coatings. Place on the tray. Repeat with the remaining truffle mix and toppings. Place the tray in the fridge for the truffles to set.
5 After 30 minutes you can pop the truffles in a box. Store in the fridge.

Lilly's tips

▶ To make vegan truffles, just use dark chocolate and replace the cream and butter with coconut oil.

Pretzel love hearts

What you'll need:

150g milk chocolate, chopped
200g pretzels
2 tbsp heart-shaped sprinkles (but any sprinkles will do!)
1 piping bag or plastic bag

If you love salty sweet treats, then these are for you! I love pretzels – they're so moreish and delicious with chocolate. These pretzel hearts are great for Valentine's lunch boxes and are ideal for kids to make themselves. Use white chocolate and different-sized pretzels to ring in the changes. I use a piping bag to pipe the chocolate into a heart shape, easily filling the inside of each pretzel. You could also make a faster version and just arrange all the pretzels tightly on a tray, use a spoon to drizzle with chocolate and scatter with the love-heart sprinkles. Equally tasty.

These are a fantastic last-minute gift idea that's not as time-consuming or fiddly as baking a cake. They do make very cute cupcake toppers, though!

Method

1 Line a tray with greaseproof paper.
2 Melt the chocolate in a heatproof bowl over a pan of simmering water.
3 Once melted, remove from the heat and set aside to cool a little.
4 If you're using a reusable piping bag, fit it with the smallest tip you have. If you're using a plastic bag, you'll need to snip the tip off once the chocolate is in the bag.
5 Stand the piping bag in a large cup and fold the sides down over the cup to hold it in place. Spoon the chocolate into the piping bag.
6 Lay all the pretzels on the tray. Carefully pipe the chocolate into the pretzels, filling in the centre and the central piece of pretzel to form a heart shape. Scatter with heart-shaped sprinkles while the chocolate is still warm. Leave to set fully before placing them in a gift box or other lidded container.

Pancake Day

What you'll need:

150g plain flour
Pinch of salt
3 eggs
420ml milk
1 tbsp sunflower oil
Butter, to cook the pancakes

Makes 6–8 large crepes

Pancake Day, also known as Shrove Tuesday, falls in February or early March and is one of my favourite days. We get to have pancakes at every meal. Sweet with lemon and sugar for breakfast, creamy sautéed mushrooms folded into pancakes for lunch, and smoked salmon with dill crème fraîche and pancakes for dinner. Yes please! Traditionally the idea was that you had to use up all your eggs and sugar as they were off limits during Lent. Nowadays, though Lent is not observed as much, Pancake Day is still going strong. I make pancakes every weekend, the thicker fluffy variety, but for Pancake Day I love a good crepe style with lemon and sugar. I've discovered the key to the perfect lacey crepe is whisking in some boiling water just before you cook them. This pancake recipe is fantastic because there's no sugar added, so you can use it as a base for your sweet or savoury creations.

Method

1 Put the flour and salt in a large mixing bowl.
2 Make a well in the centre and crack in the eggs. Pour in 100ml of the milk and the oil and start to whisk, gradually drawing in the flour. Whisk until you form a smooth, thick paste, then gradually add the remainder of the milk, whisking all the time.
3 At this point you can store the batter in the fridge till ready to use, up to 2 days.
4 Just before you begin to cook the pancakes, whisk about 3 tbsp of boiling water into the mixture. Whisk well to combine.
5 Heat a frying pan over medium-high heat.
6 Add a little butter to your pan and let it melt, tilting the pan to coat it evenly with the melted butter.
7 Add a ladle full of batter to the pan, tilting the pan to spread the batter in a thin layer.
8 Leave to cook for 30 seconds till bubbles begin to form on the surface, then loosen the edges with a palette knife and flip the pancake to cook the other side. Serve right away.

Spring clean with infused vinegar

What you'll need:

A combination of any of the following:

Citrus peel: lemon, lime, grapefruit, orange peel, with pith removed

Herbs: rosemary or thyme (fresh herbs are ideal, but dried will work too)

Spices: whole cloves, cinnamon sticks, star anise, ginger, cardamom

Plants: lavender, pine or Christmas tree sprigs, eucalyptus

500ml white vinegar
500ml water
1 spray bottle – you can reuse one from an old cleaning product, washed out very well

Makes 1 litre

A big spring clean was usually done on the eve of Imbolc. It would make sense that the house would need a good scrub with the windows open and the air flowing through after the fustiness of winter. Making your own infused cleaning vinegar is really easy and it can be scented with all sorts of delicious-smelling fragrances. It's great for cleaning, better for the environment and cuts down on unnecessary chemicals in your home. This spray is perfect for cleaning work surfaces, floors, walls, bins and sinks.

So many hardy herbs work for this. You can also add your favourite essential oils. Add a cup of this vinegar to your dishwasher in the bottom rack and run a quick cycle to clean and sanitise. You can place bread soda in your kitchen sink, then wash it down with some fragrant infused vinegar for a squeaky-clean sink and drain. Infused vinegar is also great for cleaning toilets.

Don't use this cleaner on porous stone like granite or marble.

Lilly's favourite mixes

Thieves' blend: 2 tbsp whole cloves, 2 cinnamon sticks, 2 tbsp dried lavender blossoms, 2 tbsp rosemary leaves

Festive blend: 1 tbsp whole cloves, 1 tbsp crushed cardamom pods, peel of 2 oranges, a handful of Christmas tree greenery

Summer blend: 3 tbsp lavender blossoms, peel of 2 lemons, 1 tbsp thyme leaves

Fresh blend: peel of 2 grapefruit, 4 sprigs rosemary

Method

1 Place all the fragrant ingredients you want to use in a 500ml jar.
2 Pour over the vinegar. Make sure the herbs and citrus peel are completely submerged under the vinegar.
3 Leave to infuse for one to two weeks, then strain the vinegar through a sieve into a large jug. Pop the citrus peel and herbs, etc., into the compost.
4 Add an equal quantity of water to the vinegar and transfer to a spray bottle. Keep any leftovers in a labelled jar.

Lilly's tips

▶ Add a tablespoon or two of natural soap (such as castile soap), or a natural dishwashing liquid, for even more cleaning power.

St Patrick's Day badges

What you'll need:

A4 paper or card in green, white and orange
Sellotape
Glue or stapler
Safety pins

17 March is the feast day of the patron saint of Ireland, St Patrick. St Patrick's Day is marked in Ireland and throughout the world with parades and religious or cultural events. The Chicago River is dyed green, and the Eiffel Tower in Paris is floodlit in a wash of green. When we were little, my mother would iron all of our green ribbons and my Grand-Aunt Kathleen would always provide us with a paper bag full of badges, pretty beribboned rosettes in green, white and orange. My granddad would source a big tuft of shamrock for us all to pin to our cardigans as we headed into town to watch the parade. We always brought our much-loved Irish terrier to the parade with us. She would be bedecked in green ribbons and we all took turns holding her lead. We always ate bacon, cabbage (cooked in the bacon water) and potatoes, with parsley sauce to temper the salty bacon. I still cook the same thing each year, with carrots to create the full tricolour on our dinner table.

These St Patrick's Day badges are great fun to make once you master the accordion fold – it's just like making a fan. You can make all different sizes and they're ideal for birthdays too.

Method

1 Cut two 8cm-diameter circles out to be the base and centre of your badge. Set aside.
2 Cut another piece of paper vertically into 4 equal-sized strips of 7cm x 30cm.
3 Make a series of alternating 1.5cm folds to create an accordion fold.
4 Once two strips are folded, glue or staple them together end to end.
5 Bring the other two ends together in a circle to create a rosette. Glue or staple these together.
6 You'll have to hold the rosette firmly to keep it in place.
7 Spread glue onto one circle of card and then firmly place the rosette on top. Press it down to hold it in place.
8 Write a message on the other circle and then glue it into the centre of the rosette.
9 Cut out more lengths of paper as ribbons. Glue or tape them to the back of the rosette.
10 Use a piece of Sellotape to tape the safety pin onto the back of the badge.

Woven St Patrick's Day placemats

What you'll need:

A4 construction paper in orange, green and white
Pages from magazines in coordinating colours
Scissors
Sellotape

Weaving like this is so much fun. Once you have the basic technique you can do so many variations. I love to use different widths of paper. It makes the project look much more modern and organic. Choosing patriotic colours is a fun way to dress up your dinner table on St Patrick's Day. Flick through any magazines you have for photos of the Irish landscape, the greener the better. I've used coloured construction card and some magazine images here, but you can also use felt or fabric – just sew it in place. You can make coasters to complete this table setting. Cut waves instead of straight lines from your A4 sheet for a different fun effect. Just using different shades of green can be really effective on a white tablecloth, too.

This easy craft made from basic supplies is great for so many of life's celebrations, from birthday parties to Halloween. Just choose colours that suit the occasion.

Method

1 Use one A4 piece of construction paper as the mat. Fold it in half. Cut 8 evenly-spaced slits, starting from the fold and leaving a 2cm border at the edges.

2 Cut strips 1–3cm wide and 24cm long from magazine pages/other pieces of paper.

3 Unfold the mat, then weave the paper strips over and under the slits. Fold every second one over the mat and secure all of the strips at the back with Sellotape. Ensure the strips are all snugly sitting next to one another so there are no gaps.

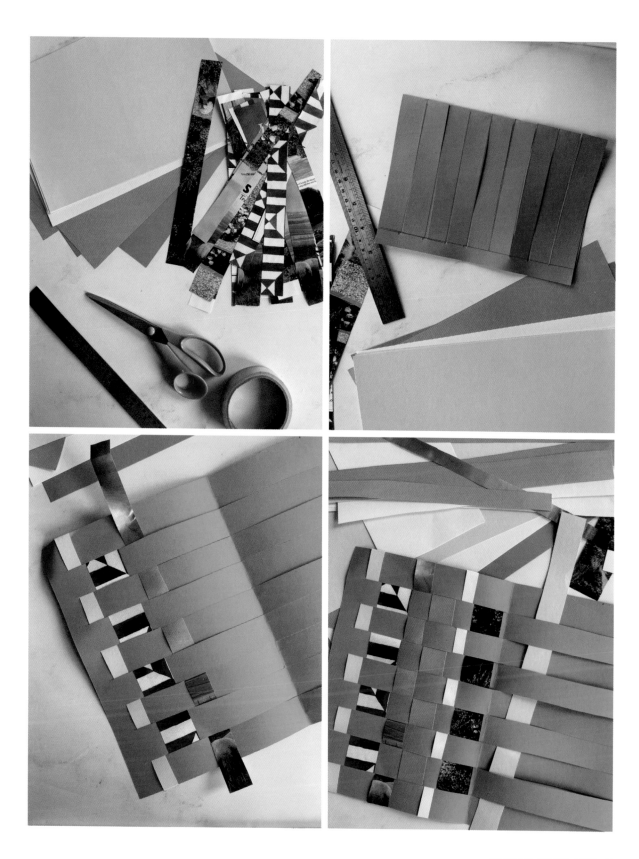

Wild garlic pesto

What you'll need:

150g wild garlic leaves (1 large handful)
70g flaked almonds, toasted (you can also use toasted sunflower seeds, cashew nuts or pine nuts)
80g Parmesan cheese, grated
300ml olive oil
Sea salt and black pepper
Lemon juice, optional

Makes 1 x 350g jar

March is the peak of wild garlic season, so look in your nearest dark, damp, leafy woodlands for some of these pretty white-belled alliums. The strong whiff of garlic should be enough to give them away – look for wide, waxy green leaves near water under shade and you'll be whipping up a batch of pesto in no time.

Wild garlic is often confused with three-cornered leeks. The leek has thin, skinny, ribbed leaves and single bell flowers, and grows absolutely everywhere in Ireland, on roadsides, in gardens and in fields. When we were little we called them onion bells. They're perfectly edible, but have more of a basic leek/onion smell than the much-sought-after wild garlic. The leaves are coarser too, but still fine for making pesto and soup. The pretty flowers are nice for decorating leek and potato soup.

I always use the flowers from wild garlic too – they are edible and make a lovely garnish. As with all foraging, only pick what you need and leave the place as you found it. Don't pick under trees (bird droppings) or in places where there's heavy traffic (car fumes), and always wash your produce well. This is a real taste of the season and something my children look forward to each year.

Method

1 Wash the wild garlic leaves well and gently pat them dry with a tea towel or dry in a salad spinner.
2 Blitz the wild garlic in a food processor until fairly smooth. You may need to add some of the oil to get it moving.
3 Add the toasted flaked almonds and the Parmesan.
4 Pour in the oil as it blends. It's nice to leave some texture, so don't blitz it too finely. Add salt, pepper and a spritz of lemon juice to taste if it needs it. Do season it very well, though.
5 Pour into jar and top with oil. Will keep in the fridge for up to 2 weeks.

Lilly's tips

▶ This pesto is amazing drizzled over pizza just out of the oven, in steak and mushroom sandwiches, swirled through soup or used to flavour cream cheese or labneh. It's perfect for salad dressings too.

Bath tea mix

What you'll need:

1 glass jar
Dried camomile (soothes muscles and calms for a healthy sleep)
Dried lavender (calming and relaxing)
Oats (soothing for dry skin, moisturising)
Linen or muslin cloth
String or twine

When my children were babies, I gave them a bath every night. It was part of their bedtime routine and, to be honest, was the only routine I did stick to! They loved splashing and playing in the bath and always emerged from the water calmer and more relaxed. Total water babies, and they still are to this day.

Lately I've been creating alternatives to the usual bubble bath with this lovely natural bath tea. It's a blend of oats, herbs and dried flowers. You can put anything into it. Mix the bath tea ingredients in equal volumes and store in a jar. To use, simply fill a muslin bag or cloth with the tea mix, then tie it up and hang onto the tap as your bath runs. Do make sure none of the mix runs down the drain. It can be disposed of in your compost bin.

Method

1 Use equal quantities of the ingredients above. Use a cup measure to portion out the same volume of oats and dried flowers. Store in a glass jar.
2 Place 3 tbsp of the oat mix into a square of cloth. Gather up the corners and tie securely with a piece of string. (Alternatively, use a small cloth bag.) This can be hung from the tap as the bath runs or left in the bath.

Lilly's tips

▶ If you've dried your own flowers, this is the perfect place for your calendula, lavender and rose petals. I love buying organic herbal teas and mixing them with the oats. Rose, camomile and peppermint are all readily available and make great additions to your bath.

Trinket dish for Mother's Day

What you'll need:

Air-drying terracotta clay
Leaves or flowers
Rolling pin
Cookie cutter
Shallow cupcake tin

Mother's Day falls on the fourth Sunday of Lent, in other words three weeks before Easter – usually the second half of March or beginning of April. Here's a very nice craft for all of those amazing mammies, which creates something as functional as it is beautiful. This air-drying terracotta clay is very handy to have for so many projects. It's widely available in art shops and online, and it's also very affordable.

I once took a night course in ceramics and really loved it. I have no patience for mastering the potter's wheel, but I loved making free-form creations. There's something very calming about working with clay, moulding it with your hands and just concentrating on what you're doing at that moment.

These lovely little trinket dishes use a cupcake tin as a mould and can be decorated using twigs, flowers or stamps. They're ideal for storing jewellery, coins or keys. The perfect little catchall for your hallway, bedroom or bathroom.

Method

1 Roll the clay out on your work surface, about 1cm thick. Place leaves or flowers onto the clay surface, and roll over them gently but firmly to make a print. Use a large cookie cutter to stamp out large discs.
2 Press the discs of clay into cupcake tins so they are moulded by the tin and will dry in that shape. After a few hours, but before they're fully set, remove the bowls, then leave to dry fully.

Lilly's tips

▶ Use any leftover clay (stored in an airtight Ziploc bag) to make Christmas decorations or the air fresheners on page 126.

Jewellery tree

What you'll need:

A handful of branches and twigs,
    strong and dry
Twine or string
Heavy bottle, vase or jar
Brown paper
Paints

I'm very disorganised, so anything that helps me to keep my things in order is a bonus! Double bonus if it's beautiful to look at. This jewellery tree is so pretty and really brightens up a desk or bedside locker. It can be whatever you need it to be: small and short for your bracelets or tall and slender for a few necklaces. If your necklaces get tangled then this jewellery tree is for you. It makes a really lovely gift come Mother's Day and can be painted any colour. Spray painting is the fast option, but I love to pick out the branches with different colours: it takes time but is fun and relaxing to do. It's a lovely project for kids to make – half the fun is rummaging around outside finding the perfect multi-stemmed branches.

Method

1 Wash the branches and scrub them well if there's any moss, etc. on them. Leave to dry completely.

2 Arrange the branches like a bunch of flowers in a pleasing tree style. Make sure it's as even as it can be on both sides, or go for a bonsai look and leave it all spread to one side.

3 Holding the bouquet of branches, begin to wrap twine tightly around the stems. Keep wrapping until they're tightly held together and then tie a knot. You can now place the 'tree' in your bottle, or wrap the base in brown paper so it fits snugly in a jar, ready for painting.

4 Choose your paints to fit in with your room decor or go for a solid, classic colour like silver, white or gold.

5 Once the wood is dry, you're ready to hang your jewellery!

Positive affirmation cards
for creativity

What you'll need:

Your favourite pen
A selection of the most important
affirmations, or you can cut out
some of mine

We all need to hear positive things about ourselves sometimes. Positive words to encourage us to keep thinking outside the box and outside our comfort zones, pushing our creative limits and making magic with a few scraps of paper and some egg boxes. The beauty of creating is in the process and not the outcome. Making things and thinking up new and beautiful ways to express ourselves is just part of life. We should encourage that any way we can.

Here are some helpful affirmations to encourage you to be creative and help you stay true to your creative self.

Make time
for things
that help
you grow

I don't
care about
perfection,
I care about
creation

Creative
people need
time to sit
around and
do nothing

'The more you
create, the
more powerful
you become.
The more you
consume, the
more powerful
others become'
James Clear

Being creative
is one of my
great joys
in life

I feel
inspired
when I make
mistakes

Method

1 Cut out the affirmations on pages 63 and 65, or compile a dozen of
  your own favourites.
2 Read the affirmations as they are or cut them out and shuffle them,
  choosing the card on top of the deck as your daily affirmation. Use
  them as mantras. Place them on your vision board. Read one while
  having your morning coffee, or carry them in your bag and read them
  when you have any spare moment in the day.

Today I am
making time
to create

My
creativity
flows freely

My
creative
energy is
limitless

I learn
and grow
from taking
creative risks

I pursue
creativity
without fear

My
creativity
helps me
connect to
the world

Easter hot cross buns

For the buns:

What you'll need:
2 tbsp (15g) active dried yeast
260g warm milk (body temperature)
70g melted salted butter, cooled
40g sugar
2 tbsp fine cut marmalade
1 egg
500g plain flour, plus extra for
   dusting the work surface
2 tsp cinnamon
2 tsp mixed spice
180g sultanas

For the crosses:

What you'll need:
50g flour
1 tbsp melted salted butter
4 tbsp water

For the glaze:

What you'll need:
100g water
75g sugar

Makes 10–12

The official date of Easter moves every year: it's the first Sunday after the full moon occurring on or after 21 March. So it could be 22 March at its earliest or 25 April at its latest. I love that it's still dictated by the full moon even though it's a Christian celebration. Either way we get to eat hot cross buns and so much chocolate. I love doing a roast leg of lamb with plenty of rosemary, minted peas and gravy. It's really lovely to have a big celebratory dinner after our Easter egg hunt in the morning.

I remember running around our garden when I was small, still in my pyjamas and dressing gown, looking for any glint of foil that would give away the chocolate's hiding place. When we were living in Zimbabwe we ran outside one Easter morning to discover that our black Labrador, Lizzy, had eaten every last piece of chocolate she could find! Amazingly, she wasn't sick after it, but we were all distraught!

Just like chocolate, hot cross buns are a must for Easter. My children love them toasted with butter and jam for breakfast. This is a really doable hot cross bun recipe. It's very easy and skips a few steps, but still results in delicious hot cross buns that are best eaten the day they're made.

Method

1 Place the yeast and warm milk in the mixing bowl of a stand mixer fitted with the dough hook. Whisk in the cooled butter and cover with a plate. Leave to stand for 5 minutes to froth up a little.
2 Add the remainder of the bun ingredients, except for the fruit. Mix for 5–6 minutes until smooth and elastic. Add the fruit, then knead for one final minute.
3 While the dough is still warm, tip it out onto a floured surface. Working quickly, divide the dough into 10–12 equal-sized pieces. Fold the corners of one dough piece in on top of itself, then flip the dough ball over and, with your hand in a claw shape, rock the dough ball in a circle shape till it forms a smooth, round ball. Repeat for the remaining pieces.
4 Place onto a lined baking tray so they are just touching. Cover with a clean tea towel and set aside somewhere warm for 15–20 minutes or till doubled in size.
5 Meanwhile mix the flour, butter and water to form a thick paste for the crosses.
6 You can also make the glaze now by simmering the water and sugar together in a small pan for 2 minutes till the sugar has dissolved and the liquid is syrupy.
7 Preheat the oven to 220°C.
8 Once the dough has risen, use a piping bag fitted with a 3mm nozzle, or with a tiny snip cut off the corner, to pipe the dough crosses onto each bun. (For instructions on filling a piping bag, see page 28.)
9 Bake for 25–30 minutes till golden brown, then brush with the sugar syrup before placing on a wire rack to cool.

Lilly's tips

▶ Any leftover syrup can be kept in the fridge for months and used to glaze other bakes or to make cocktails.

Daffodil napkin bouquet

What you'll need:

Paper or card in green, cream, orange and yellow
Glue stick
Twine or ribbon
Cloth napkins

I've really fallen in love with fabric napkins over the past few years. We always had some, but they were vintage mismatched ones that I mostly used for food styling. Then I came across Zoë Carol's beautiful everyday napkins, made from scraps of linen from her slow fashion studio in Kilkenny. These napkins are all mismatched, yet sit together so beautifully. They're just the right size and we do use them every day. I never buy paper towels so these napkins are called into action for many things. I use them to cover sourdough starter and kombucha, to line bread baskets and to wrap food. Here I've used them to create a pretty flower bouquet to grace our Easter table.

Draw your own daffodils or use real ones; the smaller 'Tête-à-tête' variety are particularly lovely for this. If using real flowers, make extra paper leaves on which to write each guest's name.

Method

1 First draw out your daffodil shapes and assemble with glue.
2 Write the name of a guest on the leaf.
3 Lay a napkin flat on the table.
4 Fold it into a triangle, then hold the triangle upright.
5 Bring the other tips into the triangle, creating a triangle tent.
6 Gather the folded napkin into a bunch near the base.
7 Place the flower onto the front of the bouquet.
8 Tie the bouquet with twine or ribbon to hold the flower in place.
9 Repeat for the other bouquets and place one on each plate.

Dyed eggs

What you'll need:

Eggs
Light-coloured crayons
3 tbsp vinegar
1 beetroot
2 tbsp turmeric
2 tbsp spirulina powder

Eggs were used to celebrate spring even in pre-Christian days, and in different cultures all over the world. The bright yellow yolk represented the sun and the new life of spring. Botanical dyes were made from onion skins and beetroot juice. I still like to use these natural dyes today, along with red cabbage, turmeric, coffee and spirulina.

Draw a design on the eggs using a light-coloured crayon. The dye will resist the crayon-coloured areas and create a pretty effect. You can also press flowers onto the eggs and hold them in place using an old pair of tights. This method leaves the imprint of the flower. Or you could use thin strips of washi tape to create a basket weave or stripes on the eggs before dipping them in the dye. Stripes can also be achieved by wrapping elastic bands around the eggs.

Method

1 Boil the eggs for about 10 minutes, then leave to cool in the water.
2 Dry the eggs well and use the crayons to draw your decorations, for example spirals and flowers.
3 Blitz the beetroot with 2 cups of water and 1 tbsp vinegar to make a vivid pink dye. Pour it into a large jar or bowl.
4 Stir the turmeric through 2 cups of water and 1 tbsp vinegar in a large jar or bowl.
5 Repeat these steps with the spirulina.
6 Divide the eggs between the three bowls or jars. Leave them to soak overnight in the dye or until you're happy with the colour.

Toadstool centrepiece

What you'll need:

3 egg boxes
Scissors
Acrylic paints
Paint brushes
PVA glue
Masking tape
A plate to use as a base (I used a wooden plate)
Moss, leaves, ferns and flowers
A little statue or toy bunny, chick or lamb

I always seem to amass a huge collection of egg boxes, especially at this time of year. I usually return the boxes to the local egg producers for reuse but there's always a few that go astray. They're ideal to use as paint palettes, with a little hollow for each colour. They're the perfect shape to make little mushrooms, too. I've used a light-up rabbit on my centrepiece here but any little toy or statue of a rabbit, chick or lamb will do. You can also just keep it to the mushrooms-and-moss woodland theme. It's all about bringing a plate of nature to the table. The texture of the egg boxes is just perfect for these adorable toadstools. There's something so magical about the fly agaric mushroom, which is native to Ireland, with its fairy-tale red cap with white freckles. As pretty as it looks, it's highly poisonous and definitely not edible. Recreating our own from unwanted cardboard finishes an Easter table so beautifully and gives it a touch of woodland magic.

Method

1   Start by cutting up the egg boxes. Cut out the little cups that hold the eggs. Then paint these red. Egg box cardboard is very porous so you may need to do two coats to get a nice strong colour. Once the red paint has dried, add the white dots. Leave to dry.
2   Cut the lids of the egg boxes in half and roll to make the mushroom stems. Glue or tape them into cylinders. Leave two flat feet at the base of each stem for taping onto the plate.
3   Arrange the stems on the plate and tape in place. Add a little PVA glue to the inside of each mushroom cap and sit it on a stem. Leave to dry.
4   Once dry, arrange moss and flowers around the mushrooms and sit the bunny, chick or lamb at the side.

Fennel and red cabbage sauerkraut

What you'll need:

2 heads red cabbage
2 ½ tbsp sea salt
2 tbsp fennel seeds
2 large Kilner jars
Small jam jar
Baking beans
1 small piece of muslin or cotton
String or elastic band

Makes 2 large jars

Back in 2014 the King of Fermentation, Sandor Katz, gave a talk at Ballymaloe Literary Festival of Food and Wine. I had already started my fermentation journey and had been tentatively making sauerkraut and water kefir. He spoke so passionately and really brought fermentation to life for me. I realised it wasn't something to be afraid of, but rather I should embrace it, have fun with it and thrive on eating it! He said to give kids fermented foods as much as possible, and he demystified it all.

Fermentation is the most low-tech thing you can do. All you need is a cabbage and some salt. Magic will happen! There are so many variations and possibilities. I'm just sharing one of my favourite basic recipes here to get your gut off to a healthy start and hopefully start a lifelong love for fermenting. It's created via lactofermentation, where the *Lactobacillus* bacteria convert naturally occurring sugars in vegetables and fruit into lactic acid. Lactic acid is a natural preservative that helps fight bad bacteria and preserves not only the flavour and texture of food but also its nutrients. Some strains support digestion and immunity.

I love eating sauerkraut with mashed potatoes and sausages or on a hot dog. It's perfect as part of a salad bowl, or as a base for coleslaw. Cheese and sauerkraut sandwiches are amazing and it's also good in wraps or burritos.

Method

1 First clean everything you'll be using really really well. You don't want to introduce any extra bacteria, so scrub your hands, chopping board, jar, etc.
2 Remove the outer leaves of the cabbage and finely shred the rest. Either use a mandoline, sharp knife or food processor.
3 Place the cabbage in a large non-metallic bowl. Pour over the sea salt and massage it all really well into the cabbage. This will break down the fibres of the cabbage and make it release its natural liquids. Add the fennel seeds and mix well.
4 Cover with a cloth and leave for an hour – you'll be amazed how much liquid will come out.
5 Pack the cabbage mixture as tightly as possible into the jars. Pack it down with your fist, and then pour the cabbage juice over the top. It's important that the cabbage is completely covered by liquid, so really press it down firmly. The more you pack it down, the more liquid it will produce, but a little cooled boiled water can be used to top it up if necessary.
6 I then add a weight to each jar. I scrub a small jam jar till spotlessly clean and fill it with baking beans, then press this down on top of the cabbage before covering.
7 Cover the top of the Kilner jar with the muslin cloth and tie with string or an elastic band. You can also put a lid on the jars, but you will have to open the lids and 'burp' them every day to release the build-up of gases once the sauerkraut starts to ferment.
8 Place somewhere cool and dark for 10–20 days. Check your sauerkraut every few days and feel free to taste it. It's essential that the cabbage stays under the water. If your kitchen is warm it might be done in a week. Once it tastes fermented enough for your liking then place it in the fridge. There may be some harmless scum or bubbles on top, so just remove that before you place it in the fridge. The sauerkraut will keep in the fridge for 1–2 months.

Lilly's tips

▶ The possibilities are endless with sauerkraut. Add grated carrot, use white cabbage, radicchio, cumin seeds, a slice of orange for flavour, coriander seeds, kohlrabi or finely sliced fennel bulbs.

Summer
Bealtaine

May, June, July

May in Ireland signals nature's blossoming. Bluebells, primroses and daisies begin to bloom.

May Day is the beginning of the old Celtic festival Bealtaine, derived from 'Bel's Fire', the fire of Belenus, Celtic God of the sun. I love that even though Christianity swept through Ireland we still maintained these pagan rituals, scattering flowers on doorsteps to keep bad fairies away and washing our faces with the morning dew. What started as the worship of the Goddess of Summer then evolved to encompass Christian traditions. The May altar for the Virgin Mary and the Queen of May procession, taking place on the first Sunday of May, are from these Christian traditions, although the May Queen is also associated with the Roman goddess Flora. It's now almost coming full circle again as we are beginning to reconnect with nature, its seasons and customs. We now pick and choose what pagan and Christian traditions we want to celebrate.

Many Irish homes, especially rurally, have strong May customs and traditions. The first day of May signals the arrival of summer and many customs revolve around protecting family, the home and livestock against supernatural forces. Farmers placed a sprig of gorse or hawthorn over the doorway of the dairy to ensure good milk supply from their cows in the summer ahead. Herbs gathered before sunrise on May Day were thought to have even better curative and restorative properties. May is everything airy-fairy so my best advice is to just embrace and enjoy it. Bonfires on May Eve and little bunches of wildflowers are a lovely way to begin the month. The yellow of the flowers symbolises the sunshine and warmth to come. Some of the ideas I suggest for celebrating the joys of summer in the pages ahead are making a beautiful flower crown on a sunny May day, harvesting wild elderflowers to make a cordial and picking purple chive flowers to infuse vinegar for salads and the winter ahead.

Midsummer is 23 June, close to the summer solstice and the longest day of the year. As with so many of these old Irish traditions, we used the light of fire to celebrate. Communal bonfires were lit on hillsides. Dancing, feasting and general merriment were features. Some of my ideas for celebrating midsummer are making a gorgeous tin can lantern to bring light into your own home, or drying herbs for winter and making beautiful flower-filled ice cubes.

July brings more projects outdoors with botanical tie-dye, flower pressing and creating your own floral essences. There's no nicer place to be than Ireland on a warm summer's day. We spend most of the summer in the garden or at the beach just enjoying these glorious months.

May flower crown for Bealtaine

What you'll need:

Long-stemmed wildflowers
Scissors
Elastic bands

May is the time of year for flower crowns, a Bealtaine tradition to celebrate and welcome summer. It's also an important month for the Catholic faith, with particular emphasis on the Virgin Mary. 'Queen of May' is sung in Catholic churches on May Day and for the rest of the month; this hymn describes crowning Mary with flowers and blossoms as Queen of the Angels and Queen of May. The tradition of making a crown of flowers for the May Queen could also have originated as a tribute to the Roman goddess Flora.

There's nothing nicer than sitting on the grass on a sun-soaked May day making daisy chains. The whole world seems to slow down around you as you pick each flower, carefully create a slit in each stem and thread a daisy through each. It's a great lesson for kids in how to pick flowers too, choosing the longest stems and leaving enough flowers behind for the bees to enjoy. To make flower crowns, however, I use a different method, braiding the long stems like a French plait, adding new flowers as it comes together.

Method

1 Pick a bunch of your favourite long-stemmed flowers. I love large daisy varieties as the stems are strong and long with bright, sturdy flowers.
2 Use an elastic band to hold three stems together just under the flower heads.
3 Start to braid the stems together and add another flower with each stem you plait, like a French plait. Curve it in a circular shape as you braid.
4 Once you've got to the length you need, shape the braided flowers into a circle and tuck the stems into the elastic band, ensuring they're held tightly.
5 You can then tuck additional flowers or leaves into any gaps, to make it full of flowers.
6 Place on your head or secure with hair clips.

Lilly's tips

▶ Your crown can also be used as a floral table centrepiece with a candle placed in the middle.

Diffuser

What you'll need:

6–8 twigs, bamboo skewers, reeds or
   dried lavender stems
An old glass bottle or ceramic vase
120ml thin carrier oil such as sweet
   almond oil or safflower
30 drops of essential oils of your
   choice
1 tbsp vodka (optional)
Decorative accents such as labels,
   fabric, twine, etc.

I have a plug-in diffuser that I really love and sometimes find myself moving it from room to room. Making your own diffuser is a really nice way to make your bedroom or bathroom smell great without needing to switch anything on. I love how it subtly scents a space through natural twigs. It looks so nice too. I always find it hard to part with pretty glass bottles, particularly the ones for balsamic vinegar. You'll need a bottle with a narrow neck that you can pack with the twigs so that none of the liquid will evaporate. You can personalise it with a label or some pretty fabric around the sides. Reeds are traditionally used but bamboo skewers or twigs work too. I sometimes use the dried-out stems from lavender once the scent has gone: just break off the flower bud on top and you're left with the perfect dried stem.

It's not necessary to use vodka, but a little alcohol does help to get the oils moving into the twigs. You could just use water and essential oils, although this will evaporate much more quickly. Either way, it's a lovely way to naturally scent your home and enjoy the benefits of aromatherapy, and it makes a beautiful gift too.

Method

1 If using twigs, you'll need to dry them first. Place them in an oven set to 120°C for an hour; this will also get rid of any bacteria. Rub off any loose bark with a tea towel.
2 Place the carrier oil in the glass bottle. Add the essential oils and vodka, if using. Swirl the bottle to mix them.
3 Arrange the twigs in the bottle so they're well spread out and not all bunched together at the base.
4 Flip the twigs over after an hour and then every few days to ensure they're soaking up the liquid and diffusing it. It will last a month.

Lilly's tips

▶ Use your favourite essential oils to spread pleasant scents around the house. Peppermint is uplifting and a mood booster, while rosemary is good for focus. Cedarwood, lemon, bergamot, vanilla, lemongrass, orange and valerian are good for stress and anxiety.

Safety note: As with all essential oils, keep out of reach of animals and children.

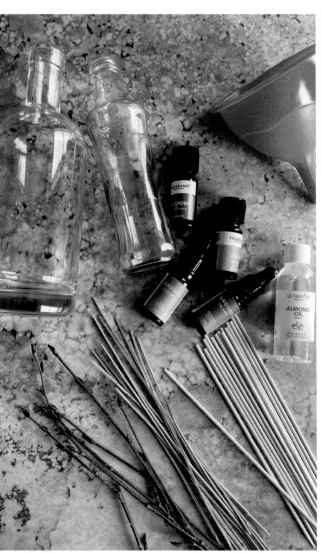

Potato printing

What you'll need:

Potatoes
A tea towel
A pencil
A small paring knife
A paintbrush
Paint
Fabric or paper to print on
Pins or masking tape

Potato printing is one of the simplest ways to start printing. All you need is a small paring knife to carve with, a potato and some paint. A wonderful rhythm develops as you load the potato with paint and stamp it down; creating patterns can be such a mindful and calming way to spend an hour or so.

It's incredibly satisfying seeing a piece of paper or blank fabric build up with your beautiful design. The negative space that's unprinted can then be filled with an extra print or painted freehand with a brush. Practise on paper to plan your design before printing on fabric. So many patterns and shapes can come from one stamp, so use them in different ways.

The best fabric to print on is cotton or linen, prewashed, clean, dry and ironed. Ensure the fabric can lie completely flat and still while you print: pin it down or use masking tape. This also helps to create a clean border. Pale fabric or paper is ideal to make your colours pop.

You can print on fabric tote bags, shopping bags, drawstring bags, napkins, sheets, pillowcases, paper, card, newspaper, brown paper, linen or cotton.

You can print with screen printing paint, chalk paints or any paint – poster paint, tester pots of emulsion, etc. For fabric, use a paint that can be heat set. Once dry, set it with a dry iron according to the manufacturer's instructions. The heat will ensure the colour sticks. It's then safe to wash.

Method

1 Cut the potato lengthways and dab it dry with a tea towel. Draw your design with a pencil on the cut side of the potato. Use a small paring knife to cut away the negative space around your design. Don't be too fussy as it's good for it to look natural – although straight edges ensure it's easier to line up the print when repeating and making a pattern.
2 Brush your paint in an even layer over the shape you've carved.
3 Press it down firmly, lift up and admire your very first print! Keep loading up the block between each print, adding a new layer of paint. Concentrate on placement and how your overall pattern will look.

May Day posies

What you'll need:

Scissors
Fresh flowers
Twine, elastic band or string

These pretty posies of seasonal flowers are usually picked the day before May Day. It's great fun for kids to make these little posies and gives them a great awareness of their surroundings, encouraging them to notice the pretty buttercups, primroses, bluebells and daisies that have popped up in their beautiful wild way again this summer. These flowers are to be placed on the doorstep or windowsill to protect the house and bring good luck. Apparently, their beauty and fragrance would distract any negative forces from entering the house. Traditionally in Ireland these little mini-bouquets would also have been left in worship of Bridget or Brigit, the pagan goddess of spring, although the focus then shifted in medieval times to encompass the Christian worship of the Virgin Mary. May altars are still a tradition in some Irish homes.

Washing your face with the morning dew that settles on the grass and flowers on May Day morning is supposed to bring great luck. Set your bare feet on the grass, close your eyes and feel grounded in the season and all that it brings. A lovely way to start any day!

Method

1 Pick flowers from the garden that are all the same length: daisies, bluebells, primroses and buttercups. A few leaves can also make their way into the bunches for structure.
2 Gather the stems halfway down and secure with a band, string or flower stem.
3 Leave on doorsteps or windowsills as a May Day gift for neighbours and friends.

Elderflower cordial

What you'll need:

30 elderflower heads
1½ litres water (boiling)
1kg sugar
Juice and zest of 4 lemons
Bottles for storage

Makes 2 litres

Elderflower cordial is the most seasonal, delightfully light drink this time of year. It's the hedgerows encapsulated in a glass. The syrup billows in a cloud when poured into water, swirling its sweet floral flavour around the glass. My children just love it – mostly because of the process.

We all head out to pick the flowers once we see the frothy cream clouds appearing on the hedges. There are elderflower trees growing all over Ireland. Try to choose some that grow away from busy traffic areas, with clean air. Look for them in a field or laneway; there may even be some in your garden. Pink elderflower tinges the cordial the most lovely blush colour. Pick the flowers on a dry day and try not to shake or disturb them too much. You want to leave as much pollen as you can on the flower heads, so handle them gently.

Make sure you add enough lemon or the cordial will be too sweet. It's delicious diluted with plain water, but can also be added to sparkling water or prosecco, or used to make cocktails or jazz up your next gin and tonic. It's also wonderful to cook gooseberries with: add a splash of cordial to a pan of topped and tailed gooseberries and leave to simmer till the berries soften and burst. Delicious with cold, softly whipped cream.

Method

1 Pick your elderflowers and remove any leaves or thick stalks. Gently lay the flowers out on a flat surface for 15 minutes to allow any bugs to escape.

2 Pour the water and sugar into a large pan, and heat gently to allow the sugar to dissolve. Remove from the heat and add the lemon juice, zest and elderflowers. Stir and cover.

3 Leave at room temperature for 24–48 hours to ensure the syrup absorbs as much flavour as possible from the flowers.

4 Strain the syrup through a sieve to remove all the flowers and zest. Pour into clean bottles and label. Cordial keeps for 4–6 weeks in the fridge once opened, or can be frozen for longer.

Chive blossom vinegar

What you'll need:

1 cup of chive blossoms
1½ cups apple cider vinegar or white vinegar
Glass jar
Glass bottle

Makes 1½ cups

The purple pom-poms that appear on the chive plant are incredibly pretty, but they also have a great subtle onion flavour. They're perfect for garnishing salads or egg salad sandwiches. Remove the individual lilac-coloured bell-shaped flowers from the flower head and scatter them wherever you need a pop of colour and flavour.

Any edible flowers or berries can be infused to flavour vinegar. Some of my favourite floral vinegars include cherry blossoms, wild garlic flowers, magnolia flowers, apple blossom, lavender, nasturtium and gorse. I also love to use herbs such as rosemary, mint, thyme, tarragon, basil, oregano or lemon balm, as well as citrus peel, garlic or ginger. It's such a great way to capture the seasons and enjoy them all year round. Before you know it, you'll have a shelf of multicoloured magical vinegars that you can reach for whenever you're cooking. The slightly gingery magnolia vinegar is a real favourite for dressing sushi rice.

I love to use this blush-pink chive blossom vinegar for salad dressings, ranch dressing, BBQ marinades, homemade mayonnaise or on roast vegetables. This vinegar will last for at least six months. It's important when straining out the flowers, or other ingredients, to remove even the smallest bits as this is what will taint your vinegar over time. So if using something fine you may need to line your sieve with a muslin cloth to ensure every last bit is removed.

Method

1 Gently crush the blossoms and pack them into a clean jar.
2 Pour over the vinegar and stir to completely cover the blossoms.
3 Cover the jar and label it.
4 Store at room temperature away from direct light and heat for
   2 weeks.
5 Strain the vinegar into a glass bottle and compost the blossoms.

Lilly's tips

▶ A faster method is to heat the vinegar to almost boiling, then pour it
   over the chive blossoms. Seal and keep for 3 days before straining.
   This gives a faster result but isn't as intensely flavoured.

The May bush or May tree

What you'll need:

Ribbons, rags and pieces of string
Scissors
A tree or bush, ideally hawthorn

The May tree was traditionally a flowering hawthorn. The tree, bush or large branch can be decorated with ribbon, string, leftover tinsel and rags. Often foil wrappers from Easter eggs are used too. It's a gaudy, bright and glittery feature in the garden that's most welcome after a dark winter. It's thought to bring good luck for the year ahead and serve as a type of protection from mischievous fairies that were out and about on May Eve. It always reminds me of our birthday parties when we were little and a lollipop tree would take centre stage. Similar to this, a lollipop tree is a branch stuck in a pot that we adorned with lollipops tied with ribbon to each little branch. Sweet in every way!

If you are tying ribbon to the tree, try to use something that will biodegrade naturally or simply remove the ribbons once the month is over. Keep the ribbons on for the entire month to ensure luck and good health for you, your family and your cattle, if you happen to have some!

Method

1 Cut your ribbons and pieces of string into similar lengths.
2 Tie them to the branches of the tree.
3 Remove them once the month is over.

Summer solstice lanterns

What you'll need:

Empty tin can (remove label and clean)
1 heavy kitchen cloth or towel
Nail
Hammer
Wire, to make a handle
Wire cutter
Pliers
Spray paint
Sand or pebbles for weight
Candles (you could also use solar candles)

21 June has the longest day and the shortest night of the year. No matter how separate we are from nature and the world around us, when we feel the warmth of the sun at its most potent we are no longer separated from our environment. We cannot be immune to the abundance of light, heat and energy peaking in our natural world.

Our Celtic ancestors saw this as a time of blooming, blossoming and wild abandon. The appreciation of and reliance on the sun to grow our crops is what made our ancestors so close to nature and aware of seasons changing. Usually huge bonfires were lit to celebrate the sun, but a safer way to celebrate nowadays in your own home is to make these lovely lanterns, with a spiral design inspired by my trip to Newgrange when I was in secondary school.

Newgrange is best known for the illumination of its passage and chamber by the winter solstice sun. Spiral designs are chiselled into large rocks and walls around the monument.

These lanterns are a great way to recycle tin cans and are perfect for outdoor barbecues, or just nights when you're sitting outside chatting as the sun goes down.

Method

1 Fill the can with water and freeze until solid. This step means that when you're hammering the tin it won't buckle and the tin will stay in shape.
2 Cradle the frozen tin in the cloth, flat on a table. Hammer out your design by tapping the nail through the tin. You can draw a design on or just work freehand. Punch two holes on opposite sides near the rim if you want to add a handle.
3 Run the tin under hot water to loosen and remove the ice.
4 To make a handle, snip a length of wire and attach it to the can through the two holes near the rim. Use pliers if needed to crimp the ends closed.
5 Paint the can in your chosen colour.
6 Add a few tablespoons of sand or a few pebbles to the tin to weigh it down and place a candle inside.

Lilly's tips

▶ Use citronella candles to keep unwanted insects away. You can also make seasonal versions of these lanterns with snowflake designs, autumn leaves, Easter eggs, etc.

Rosewater

What you'll need:

4–6 freshly picked chemical-free
    rose heads
Sheet of paper
A large saucepan and lid
1 jar lid
1 small heatproof bowl
Ice packs or ice cubes
Glass bottle or jar, or spritz bottle if
    desired

There's something so intoxicating about the smell of roses. Real roses, freshly picked, still warm from the sun. I just can't get enough of that smell. A Persian scientist is said to have first discovered rosewater in the tenth century and Iran is still famous for its mass production of this special scented water, which is made using steam distillation. The good news is that you can also make it at home. All you need are roses that you know to be chemical-free.

Rosewater has many benefits: it's a great toner, is anti-inflammatory and can calm your skin. It also hydrates your skin and makes a lovely refreshing spritz throughout the day. One of my favourite ways to use it is when I'm ironing clothes. Add it to the water chamber of your iron and it will puff out floral steam. Or spritz your bedclothes: wrinkles will loosen out (especially handy for linen sheets) and your bed will smell like a bed of roses!

Method

1 First remove all the petals from the rose heads and spread the petals on the paper to allow any bugs to escape. Discard the stems and any green leaves.

2 Place the jar lid in the saucepan. Place the bowl on top. The bowl will catch all the distilled rosewater.

3 Scatter the rose petals into the saucepan around the bowl. Add just enough water to cover the petals.

4 Bring the water to the boil over a medium-high heat, then turn down to a gentle simmer and place the saucepan lid on upside down. This will cause the water to drip down into the bowl.

5 Place the ice cubes or ice pack on top of the lid to accelerate the process.

6 After 30 minutes of simmering, carefully remove the ice packs and lift the lid. If there's only a small amount of water in the bowl, replace the lid and leave it to simmer longer. It can take up to 2 hours.

7 Very carefully remove the bowl and leave to cool. Transfer the rosewater to a clean glass bottle or jar. It will last for up to 3 months. When using it as a facial spritz I like to keep it in the fridge.

Father's Day clay air freshener

What you'll need:

Air-drying terracotta clay (available in art shops)
Rolling pin
Cookie cutters
Letter stamper
Natural elements to stamp and make impressions with such as flowers, twigs, leaves, etc.
Pencil
Greaseproof paper
Ribbon or twine
Essential oils or cologne

This is a cute and easy craft that always has such lovely results. I have these clay air fresheners in my car and in my wardrobe too. You can use anything to make prints in the clay. I love using flowers and twigs, letter stampers to personalise them and cookie cutters to shape them. They're the perfect gift for Father's Day, the third Sunday of June, and you can spray them with cologne or use essential oils. The clay is so absorbent and ideal for this.

I really love ceramics, the look and the feel. I love that handmade ceramics started with an idea and were then brought to life by a person's hands. I once did an eight-week ceramics course by night when Hazel was a small baby. It was great to go to the cold studio on a winter's night and sit by the stove and make things. Having spent all day with three kids under the age of four, it was lovely to just sit and create something with my own hands. I made a few things, including a butter dish that we still use to this day.

Method

1 Roll the clay out till it's 2.5cm thick. Stamp your clay circles out using the cookie cutters. Space them closely together to avoid waste. Use stamps or flowers to create patterns on the discs. Poke a hole in the top of each disc with a pencil if you want to hang them.

2 Leave them to dry on greaseproof paper, then transfer to a wire rack after a few hours. After a few days they will be completely dry.

3 String a ribbon or twine through the hole in each disc and create a loop for hanging.

4 Add a few drops of essential oils or a spray of cologne to the back of each clay disc. Top up the scent every few weeks.

Hammered flower fabric table runner

What you'll need:

Colourful flowers such as rose petals, pansies, calendula, dandelions
Light-coloured natural fabric (cotton or linen)
Cardboard
Masking tape
1 A4 sheet of paper
A rubber mallet hammer
An iron

This is a fun project that involves a roam around outdoors. Pick the most colourful seasonal flowers you can find; choose flowers with thin petals. Rose petals, pansies and calendula are all bright and in full bloom. You can then transfer these beautiful flowers onto the fabric and make a very pretty table runner. The colour from the flower transfers like splattered watercolour paint onto the fabric to give a very delicate, pretty result. These colours will fade when you wash the fabric, so try to avoid having to do so – just spot clean where you need to. This is a lovely way to make use of special bright bouquets from Valentine's Day or birthdays, the memorable bunches that you don't want to forget. It is a nice alternative to drying the bouquets, and the fabric can be framed or used to make a cushion cover.

This is an easy craft for kids to do outdoors but can also be a rewarding project for adults. The end result really is so pretty and can be done to suit whatever occasion, be it birthday parties, Sunday lunch or Easter brunch.

Method

1 Pick the petals from the rosebuds and other flowers, or use the flower heads whole, depending on what look you're going for. Ensure all the flowers are flat and thin for best results.

2 Tape the fabric to the cardboard to avoid wrinkles and hold it in place. Arrange the flowers or petals on the fabric, face side down. It's best to do this on the ground outdoors, somewhere flat and stable. You'll have to hammer quite hard to get results, so keep that in mind!

3 Place the paper over the flowers, then hammer down on a flower to transfer the pigment. Keep pounding until the paper becomes wet with the hammered flower. Remove the paper and flower to admire your work. Repeat with the remaining flowers to create a pattern you like.

4 Once you're happy with the final design you can remove the cardboard, then flip the fabric over so that the hammered side is flat against the cardboard. Iron on a low heat to set the colours.

Drying herbs for winter

What you'll need:

Leafy herbs such as oregano
Scissors or garden shears
Salad spinner or clean tea towel
Twine for hanging the herbs
Jam jars, to store the dried herbs

I use so many herbs during the summer months and grow quite reliant on having fresh tarragon and parsley so readily at hand. Steeping mint leaves in hot water for tea, tucking rosemary into a leg of lamb, plenty of sage and thyme for stuffing and oregano in all manner of tomato sauces. Once you begin to use fresh homegrown herbs it's very hard to do without them. Oregano seems to be a plant that thrives in our coastal, south-facing garden; even though it gets battered by sea air, it grows so well. It's also the herb I find most use for as it's so versatile. So it makes sense to dry this in abundance and ensure I can use it all through the winter months too. This is a guide for harvesting and drying oregano but it's the same basic method for so many types of herb such as thyme, rosemary, verbena or lemon balm.

Method

1 Harvest the oregano before it comes into flower. This is when the flavour and oils are most potent. If it has flowered you can still pick and dry the leaves, but it will be less intense.

2 Harvest once it reaches 15cm tall. You can harvest it quite regularly all summer long once the plant is mature and established. This will encourage even more leaf growth and will prevent it from going to bloom and seed too early.

3 Wash the oregano and remove any insects and any yellowing or damaged leaves.

4 Dry really well in a salad spinner or by blotting dry with a tea towel, then leave to air-dry on a rack for an hour or so.

5 Tie into small bunches (so they will dry faster) and hang somewhere cool and dark with good air circulation. It usually takes 2 weeks for these little bunches to fully dry out. The leaves will crumble to the touch once they're ready.

6 Carefully strip the leaves from the stems, discard the stems and store the leaves in an airtight jar. Store somewhere dry and dark to increase their shelf life.

Floral ice cubes

What you'll need:

Edible flowers: calendula, primrose, daisies, borage, scented geranium, rose, cornflower, fuchsia
Piece of paper
Ice cube trays
Water

There are so many edible flowers that grow well here in Ireland. Each little petal and flower head can be added to ice cubes, providing a little pop of colour to adorn any drinks party or barbecue. This is a really easy and rewarding project for kids. They can help identify and pick the flowers, then assemble them indoors. It's truly magic coming across some of these flower ice cubes during the winter months, those pretty flowers preserved perfectly inside. I've always loved flowers floating in water and floating candles. I think it was probably a very 1990s trend that I thought was just the epitome of elegance and how I imagined being a grownup would be. My house would be filled with bowls of floating candles and camellias. And, well, it has almost turned out like that.

Method

1 Pick all the flowers, then spread them on a piece of paper and leave for an hour or so to allow any bugs to escape.
2 Depending on the flowers, you could pop an entire flower head into each ice cube or just a mixture of petals. Top up the ice cube trays with water and freeze till solid.
3 These are beautiful when piled high in a bowl and served on a drinks tray, in cocktails or in a large glass jug of water.

Lilly's tips

▶ You can use the same principle to make an ice bowl by putting a smaller bowl inside a larger bowl. Use ice cubes as a buffer between them, then fill the gaps with flowers and water, and place in the freezer. Release the bowls once frozen by running them quickly under a warm tap. It's a really stunning way to serve ice cream during the summer months. Come winter you can use cranberries, star anise, herbs or orange peel. The possibilities are endless!

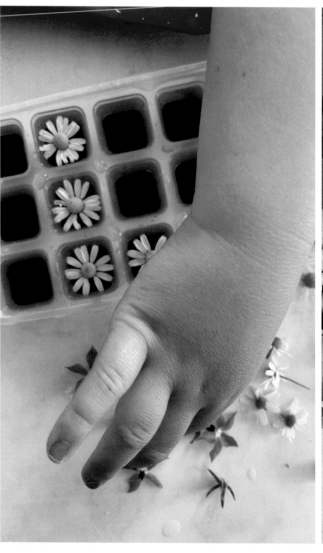

Drying lavender

What you'll need:

Fresh lavender stems
Scissors or garden pruners
Twine or elastic bands for tying
A jar or brown paper bag, to store
  the dried lavender

I absolutely love French lavender. Any time of year when I smell lavender, I'm just transported to the garden on a hot summer day as the cat brushes past the lavender bushes lining the steps. That area of the garden is always alive with bees hovering from stem to stem. I love to leave the flowers long enough for nature's harvesters to take what they need before I cut them. I only cut a few stems at a time and dry what I need. They're beautiful to have in the house, subtly scenting bedrooms with their distinctive perfume.

I once visited a therapeutic herb garden in Switzerland, and it was incredible to walk around and take in all the smells and textures. There were so many amazing smells condensed into such a small space, it really was incredible. I knew then that when I had my own garden I'd recreate that feeling of abundance with beneficial herbs, so my own children could experience how a whole row of lavender smells on a warm summer's day.

Once your lavender is dried, you could try making lavender packs that can be kept in drawers with clothes or stored in shoes – it's a great project for using up old fabric scraps and they smell so lovely!

Method

1 Cut the flowers at the base of the stem; use a sharp scissors or pruners to snip them. The flower bud has the highest concentration of essential oils so is the most fragrant part of the plant. It's best to dry with the leaves and stems intact, though, as it will make the finished product more versatile. You can then shake off the buds or display the whole stems in vases or floral arrangements.
2 Make small bunches of 15–20 stems, tied loosely to avoid moisture build-up.
3 Hang the bunches upside down in a cool dry place, out of direct sunlight. I hang them in the kitchen on the back of the door. That way I can check them each day as I pass to make sure they're drying evenly. It's important to let air circulate around them.
4 Once dried, store in an airtight container in a dark place so they keep their scent and colour. A large Mason jar is ideal.
5 I usually only pick what I need and leave the rest for the pollinators. One bunch a week during lavender season is all I need to ensure a supply of beautifully fragranced stems to use all winter long for different projects, or just for display.

Lilly's tips

▶ The best time to cut the flowers for drying is just before they open into full bloom. You can still use them after this, but they may lose their colour and be less potent.

Floral essences

What you'll need:

Flowers of choice
A glass bowl
Spring water
A leaf
A large glass jar
Brandy
Small brown glass dropper bottles (reuse ones you already have or buy online)

Now here's where things may get a bit too hippy-dippy for you. But look, just trust me. It's fun, it's lovely and have you heard of Bach's Rescue Remedy? Well, that's a floral essence. Often confused with essential oils, these little bottles smell like brandy and they contain the much-diluted essence or the energy of the flower. I had a little bottle of Rescue Remedy, a mix of five plant essences, in my schoolbag as I sat my Leaving Certificate exams. I remember taking a few drops and breathing deeply before entering the exam hall for each exam. It definitely helped me to feel in the moment and calm. Being able to regain some control in an unpredictable exam situation is invaluable.

It does have a very 'Emperor's New Clothes' feeling about it but the ritual, when done sincerely, is undeniably grounding and so helpful. Dr Edward Bach, a physician and homeopath, developed the plant- and flower-based essences in the 1930s. He spent many years in the Bach Centre in Oxfordshire, England, exploring the use of flowers and plants. He developed a gentle system of 38 flower essences, and plants from that very garden are still used today to make Bach's formulas exactly as he did. The flower's energy is extracted through the light of the sun, but this can also be done by bright moonlight.

Just think of it as a talisman. When you take a drop of the liquid it grounds you in the moment: you acknowledge how you're feeling, breathe deeply and recharge with the vibrations of the flowers. For me part of the process is actually making the essences. It's the perfect thing to do on a sunny weekend. Choose your flowers, take your time and just be in the moment.

What flowers can help with

Borage: heavy heart, grief, lack of courage

Blackberry: procrastination

Buttercup: low self-worth, self-deprecating

Calendula: argumentative

Camomile: moody, irritable, unable to release emotional tension

Cosmos: overwhelmed, unfocused

Dandelion: tense, over-striving, hard-driving

Dill: overwhelmed, hypersensitive

Fuchsia: hyperemotionality, hysteria

Gorse: pessimism, defeatism, inability to trust

Heather: talkative, self-absorbed

Honeysuckle: nostalgic, emotional attachment to the past

Lavender: nervous, highly strung, insomnia

Nasturtium: depletion of life force due to too much study

Oak: iron will, taking on too much

Olive: exhaustion, inability to rest

Peppermint: dull or sluggish

Red Clover: susceptible to panic or anxiety

Rosemary: forgetfulness, poor learning ability

Sage: seeing life as ill-fated

Method

1 On a very sunny day decide which flowers you'd like to use. Whichever ones you feel drawn to and that interest you are usually best.
2 Fill your glass bowl with water and place it in full direct sunlight.
3 Use a leaf to pick the flowers so that none of your own energy will be in the mix.
4 Float the flowers in the bowl of water, covering the surface with flowers.
5 Only pick as much as you need from the plant, and take a moment to be grateful that it's blooming so beautifully and that you have access to it (this is all part of the grounding ritual).
6 Now leave that bowl of floating flowers in full sun and make sure your shadow does not cross it. Leave for 3–4 hours so the sun's rays can warm the water and shine through the flowers, infusing the water with energy.
7 Once the flowers have infused, use a leaf to remove each flower. They can be composted or returned to the earth near the original plant.
8 Pour the infused water into a clean glass jar. Add an equal amount of brandy to make a 50:50 dilution. Label this jar with plant name, dilution rate and bottling date. Store in a cool, dark place. It will last 4–5 years. This is the mother essence.
9 To make a daughter essence we dilute it once again. Add 5 drops of mother essence to a 30ml dropper bottle. Fill the remainder of the bottle with a 50:50 mix of water and brandy.

Lilly's tips

How to use floral essences:
▶ Place a drop or two of the daughter essence on your tongue.
▶ Add a few drops to your bottle of water to sip during the day.
▶ Apply to acupuncture points or chakras.
▶ Use as a spray or mist in your home.
▶ Add several drops to your bath.

Paper cutlery holder made from school art

What you'll need:

A4 or square sheets of paper or drawings
Scissors
Glue stick
Sellotape

I find it incredibly difficult to part with any drawings or artwork that my children have done. I just love them. My eldest, Liam, is now 10 so you can imagine the collection I've amassed. He loves to draw and is very prolific, writing comic books and designing characters and storyboards for his animations. Cathal has a different style: large, detailed black and white drawings, using every inch of space on the page. There's always so much happening in his technical drawings, so much humour and action in those details. Hazel draws characters with huge eyes, a whole rainbow of colours and lots of emotion in every line of that pencil. I used to love looking through all of our own artwork when we were little and always appreciated that my parents kept so much of it despite there being eight of us! So in an effort to maximise their efforts we started making little cutlery holders from their coloured pages back in playschool and we still make them. Reusable, unique and a great way to appreciate their handiwork. These make lovely presents too, if you can bear to part with them!

Method

1 If the drawing is on a rectangular page, cut it into a square.
2 Fold the paper in half and half again lengthways to crease it.
3 Unfold the paper and proceed as follows.
4 Use the creases as a guide. Fold a small triangle down on the top left-hand corner of the first rectangle till it meets the first crease.
5 On the opposite side fold the far right-hand corner down into a larger triangle to meet the middle of the second crease.
6 Then fold the first fold over, followed by the last fold, as per the photos.
7 Use a little glue to keep the folds in place.
8 Once assembled, fold the end up, then fasten with a piece of sticky tape so the cutlery doesn't fall out.

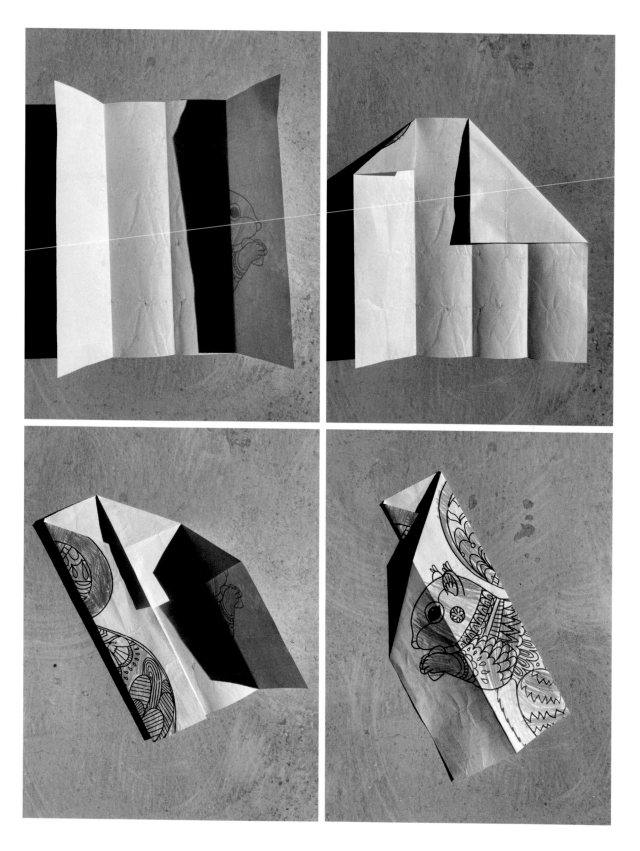

Flower pressing

What you'll need:

Flat flowers or buds, dry
A very heavy book OR a flower press
Sheets of blotting paper

I always had a flower press when I was a child. I think I first got one when we lived in Zimbabwe. We had no TV but loads of different hobbies, from keeping silkworms in shoe boxes to trading scented papers in school. We all loved skipping, playing rounders and pressing flowers. I wish I'd kept some of the flowers I pressed over the years in our African garden. Now I show my kids how to preserve flowers from our own garden or memorable trips to West Cork, where we spent the day hiking all over Bere Island with my sister Maeve, admiring the fuchsia and montbretia as we went.

You can use heavy books lined with blotting paper or use a flower press. You can also use a hot iron, turn the steam off and press down on the flowers between two sheets of paper till dried. There are so many different ways to use the resulting flowers. You can glue them to bookmarks, cards or headed paper, or make art and frame them behind glass to preserve them. Place them in your transparent plastic phone case to see them every day. Single flowers can make an impact on a card or note, but combining them in a dried bouquet can look spectacular too.

Method

1. Choose flat, bright flowers in full bloom or buds, depending on what effect you're going for.
2. Place your chosen flowers between two pieces of paper and place inside a book or flower press. I usually do pages of the same flower. Ensure they don't overlap or touch one another.
3. Weigh the book down with something heavy. Weights are ideal, or more heavy books.
4. You may need to change the paper every three days or so. Check their progress.
5. After 2–3 weeks the flowers will be completely dry. I like to leave them on the paper until I want to use them.
6. Carefully remove the flowers from the paper when ready to use: they're quite delicate.

Lilly's tips

▶ The flowers are delicate so don't apply glue directly to them. Instead place glue on the card before pressing the flower in place. Any dried flowers that do tear or break can be used to make paper. This organic matter gives beautiful textural results.

Pink lemonade

What you'll need:

3 lemons
3 tbsp sugar
Handful of raspberries, if using
250ml water
Mint sprigs, to garnish
A sharp paring knife
Nutribullet or similar high-speed
   blender

This is without a doubt the easiest method for making lemonade. Over the years I've learned all sorts of syrup-making, juicing and so on, but this method comes from Jordan. I took a cookery class in Beit Sitti; it literally translates as 'our grandma's place'. It's a cookery school run by three sisters, teaching the best authentic Palestinian and Jordanian recipes, and local grandmothers teach the classes. We had a wonderful afternoon there learning how to make flatbread, the most delicious chicken moutabel and this lemonade, among other things. They added mint to theirs to make it extra refreshing. This is super simple to make with kids. Use any citrus: blood orange makes a dramatic winter version and limes are delicious too. I make my lemonade pink by adding a few raspberries – they also give a delicious flavour – but you can leave these out if you'd prefer to stick with the good old original. This lemonade is best enjoyed well chilled the day it's made. Pour into a bottle and give it a good shake before serving.

Method

1 Peel the lemons using a sharp paring knife. (You can zest the citrus first and freeze the zest for use in other recipes.) Slice the lemons thickly and remove the seeds. Add the lemon slices to the cup of a high-speed blender.
2 Add the sugar and a few raspberries, if using. Top up with the water and blitz till smooth.
3 Pour through a sieve and discard the resulting pulp.
4 Pour into a bottle or jug and chill before serving with ice and a sprig of mint. You can dilute it further or serve as is. Add a few floral ice cubes from page 139 for an even prettier glass.

Tie-dye

What you'll need:

White cotton fabric
Rubber bands
White vinegar, to use as a fixative
Pot and pans, large bowls
Raw materials to make your natural
   dye, as follows:
Pink: raw beetroot, red onion skins,
   hibiscus flowers
Peach: avocado skins and pits
Yellow: onion skins, turmeric
Blue: elderberries
Green: grass, spinach, spirulina
Purple/blue: red cabbage
Brown: coffee grounds

Can tie-dye please never go out of fashion?! It's so much fun. In school I loved batik-making – painting wax on fabric then dyeing the fabric. Tie-dye has a similar feel, working with the negative space on the fabric to make patterns. It's so much fun to see the results, different every time. You can use string or elastic bands to tie up the fabric. I always have a stash of elastic bands in my kitchen from produce like spring onions or asparagus. It's worth holding on to them and you'll never need to buy elastic bands again! I love experimenting with natural dyes, from earthy onion skin to pink beetroot to bright yellow turmeric. It's all very safe for kids to handle once cooled, and is a lovely project to do outdoors when the sun is shining. Look for faded white clothes in charity shops or your own wardrobe that could do with a makeover. We usually use the old polo shirts from school to give them a new lease of life for summer while they still fit!

Method

1 First prepare your fabric for dyeing. Mix 1 part vinegar to 4 parts water in a large pot. Simmer all your fabric in this for one hour prior to using. Then run the fabric under cold water and wring out the excess.

2 Use rubber bands to twist sections of the fabric and tie them up. The folds and creases will remain white while the rest of the fabric will be dyed.

3 While the fabric is simmering, make your dye. Mix one part raw ingredients (so 1 cup of shredded red cabbage, for example) with two parts water (2 cups water). Use 1 tbsp ground turmeric or spirulina to 2 cups of water. Bring the mix to a boil and simmer for 1 hour to achieve an intense colour. Next strain out the vegetables or onion skins, etc., so you're left with the coloured water.

4 Immerse the fabric into the coloured water and leave it to sit until you're happy with the resulting colour, for an hour or as long as overnight. Some dyes will work faster than others; turmeric is very fast, while spirulina is slower.

5 Pull out the fabric and rinse it in cold water. Remove the rubber bands and hang the fabric to dry.

Autumn
Lúnasa

August, September, October

Lúnasa marks the onset of August, autumn and the harvest season, and is traditionally celebrated on 1 August or the first Sunday in August. Food features strongly in Lúnasa festivities, and rituals typically centre on the assurance of abundance as the harvest provides plenty of new crops, freshly baked bread and just-picked berries. Lúnasa is Mother Nature's call to us to look at the abundance around us, and it's a key tradition that we celebrate this with great joy. My own birthday is on 1 August and I'm very food-focused, always eager to provide a feast, and I just love hosting events and celebrating all that we can. It never really struck me until researching this book that it could be tied to the season in which I was born. August in Ireland still feels quite like summer, with warm weather and long evenings.

Once autumn arrives and the temperatures start to dip, I find hibernation really begins to kick in. Those bright pink sunrises and dramatic night skies with the light low on the horizon. It's that distinctive September sun, defiant and pure against the last of the blowsy summer flowers as the petals begin to drift off. Some of the best sunrises and sunsets happen in autumn.

As Halloween, or Oíche Shamhna, approaches, the mornings and evenings become so much darker. Already my children are talking about possible costumes, face paints, hairstyles and trick-or-treat bags. Routes they'll walk this year, torches they'll take and sweets they'll receive.

When we were little, we used to cut up cereal boxes to make masks, stuff black tights with balls of newspaper to make cats' tails and transform into ghosts with puffs of baby powder all over our faces in a cloud of talc. We always loved to do some traditional games at night too – bobbing for apples, snap apple and cutting the barmbrack. Nowadays we always end up with monkey nuts scattered all over the kitchen table as the children tip out their loot after spending the evening trick-or-treating. Various swaps and bargaining take place before we start the Halloween games and then watch a movie. *Hocus Pocus* is always such a classic, with just the right amount of scare and fun for younger kids.

I love using pumpkins as decorations around the house. They look fantastic piled high on the mantelpiece or doorstep. I love how they grow so well here in Ireland, look so fantastic and we get to eat them too! My own kids want to carve every pumpkin they see as soon as they get it. But pumpkin carving is best left for the last week before Halloween, especially if you're keeping the pumpkin indoors in the warmth. I love adding a burst of gold spray paint – it just transforms everything and adds a touch of glittery magic.

Halloween also marks the transition point between autumn and winter. Once the clocks go back at the end of daylight saving time it's like flicking a switch. We're into winter all of a sudden, the temperatures drop, light fades. It's dark by late afternoon and I find myself making more soup. This time of year always marks the start of the hot chocolate season, too. We used to always have it with cream crackers after school when I was little. I used to love watching the golden butter melt and pool on the surface of the hot chocolate as I dipped in the crackers. My own little cacao ritual in 1980s rural Ireland!

Baking bread to celebrate Lúnasa

To make your sourdough starter

What you'll need:
100g wholegrain rye or wheat flour
100ml cooled boiled water per day
1 large wide-mouthed jar or container
1 square of muslin or other cotton cloth
2 elastic bands
500g strong white bread flour, for feeding the starter

To make 2 loaves

What you'll need:
150g sourdough starter
850g strong white bread flour, plus extra for dusting
630ml warm water
100g fine porridge oats
15g fine salt
A little olive oil for greasing
2 round, lidded Pyrex dishes or cast-iron pots with lids
Greaseproof paper

Lúnasa is mentioned in some of the earliest Irish literature and has pagan origins. Traditionally people walked up mountains or to the tops of hills, Croagh Patrick being a popular pilgrimage to this day. They picked bilberries, little wild blueberries, and made them into cakes. They took part in athletic contests and activities (most notably the Tailteann games, like the Irish Olympics) that honoured the warrior god Lugh; his name means 'light' or 'brightness'. The first of the corn was cut and little dolls were made from the husks.

It's the perfect time of year to bake bread and celebrate the harvest!

When I did the three-month cookery course in Ballymaloe Cookery School I mastered yeast bread, but never really had the patience for sourdough. Some years later I did a hands-on sourdough course with Joe Fitzmaurice in Riot Rye in Cloughjordan. I really recommend it. That gave me confidence to give sourdough another go and helped me to understand wild yeasts a little better. But, like all things, what I really needed to do was just get started. So over the past four years I've been baking sourdough my own way and discovering what works for me. I have a very easy, hands-off method that I'm delighted to finally share in this book!

Bread-baking is one of the most rewarding skills you can learn: transforming water, salt and flour into a lifegiving loaf. Sourdough is much easier to digest than soda bread or commercial yeast bread; it's full of flavour, more nutritious and it supports gut health. The fermentation process improves the bioavailability of minerals, vitamins and fibre.

Sourdough takes patience. Your sourdough starter will bake better bread as it matures and so will you. Each loaf you bake is a step towards better bread. First, you'll need to make a sourdough starter using wholemeal rye flour and water, which takes one week to develop. My basic method is below.

Method – sourdough starter

- **Day 1:** Mix the wholegrain flour with 100ml water till smooth and place in the jar. Cover with the cloth and secure the cloth with an elastic band. Leave to sit at room temperature for 24–48 hours, until you see bubbles forming.
- **Day 2:** Once you see some bubbles forming it's time to discard all but 50g starter and add 100g strong bread flour and 100ml cooled water. Cover and set aside for 24 hours.
- **Day 3:** It should be bubbling nicely by now. Again, discard all but 50g and feed with 100g strong flour and 100ml cooled water. Cover and set aside. Place an elastic band around the outside of the jar to show the level of the starter. This way you can track its activity and see when it's risen and grown or when it's collapsing down. Feed it after it's peaked and it becomes more liquid: when it's hungry.
- **Days 4, 5 and 6** are all repeating the process above. Hopefully by now it'll be lively, bubbling and ready to bake with. On Day 6, do not discard your extra starter, as you will need 150g of it to bake your bread.

Method – baking sourdough

1. The night before you want to bake, feed your 150g starter with 150g strong flour and 150ml warm water. Stir together till smooth, then cover with a cloth. Leave at room temperature overnight. In the morning do the float test to see if your starter is ready to work with: place 1 tsp starter into a glass of water, and if it floats then it's ready! If you see that the starter has risen and then collapsed, you may have missed your window. It's better to catch the starter on the way up when it's liveliest rather than on the way down before it sinks. If this happens, see the tip below for what to do.
2. I use a stand mixer and dough hook to make this bread; it can also be mixed by hand but is quite a wet dough to work with. Place 300g of your starter mix into the mixing bowl. Keep the remaining 150g for your next batch of bread.
3. Add 480ml warm water and mix well. Next add 100g fine porridge oats and mix till combined. Finally add 700g strong bread flour. Mix till this is roughly combined, then cover with a cloth and leave to rest for 30 minutes.
4. Next add 15g fine salt and mix for 5 mins till smooth. Oil a large bowl with a little olive oil and tip the dough in, cover with a cloth or plate and leave to rise for 4–6 hours till almost doubled in size. You'll know it's ready when you press your finger in the dough and it slowly rises back up.
5. Tip the dough onto a lightly floured surface. Divide in half, then stretch each piece into a rectangle. Fold down the top third of each rectangle. Fold up the bottom third and then pull each corner together, tucking in any corners as you turn the dough.
6. This will all help to trap air and increase surface tension. Try not to burst any bubbles that may have formed in the dough. Use a light touch.
7. Place each dough ball in a Pyrex dish or cast-iron pot lined with greaseproof paper. Now leave the dough to prove for 2–3 hrs.

Generally, at room temperature, it takes half the time of the first proving. (However, I like to prove my dough in the fridge overnight once it's shaped. A long, slow, cold ferment. You can leave it there for as long as 48 hrs, and bake it straight from the fridge for a better rise.) When you're ready to bake, preheat the oven to 240°C. Dust the tops of the loaves with flour and score using a sharp knife; you can also cut into them using a scissors. Place the lids on to trap the moisture, bake for 40 mins, then remove the lids and bake for a further 10–15 mins till the loaves have gone a nice dark colour. If they're too crusty for your liking, wrap in tea towels for the steam to soften the crust as they cool. Leave to cool on a wire rack for 1 hour before cutting.

Lilly's tips

▶ Here's what to do if your starter has collapsed before you get a chance to bake with it. Discard 300g of the starter; there are plenty of recipes and ideas for how to use discard, or you can compost it. Feed the remaining 150g of starter with 150g strong flour and 150g warm water in order to bake the next day. Watch the starter rise and catch it on the way up while it's liveliest. Repeat the float test before proceeding.

Herb bundles

What you'll need:

Dried sage leaves (to cleanse and purify)
Dried lavender (for restfulness)
Dried rose petals (for love and luck)
Dried rosemary (for mental stimulation)
Cotton twine
Scissors
Heatproof bowl or shell
Matches

We have a long history of symbolic smoke and fire rituals in Ireland. During Bealtaine, cattle would be driven between two smoking bonfires or through smoking embers on May Day. This was to protect the cattle from disease, to cleanse them and to encourage good milk supply. When the bonfires died down, people would take the ashes and sprinkle them over the crops and livestock. Herbs were relied on for poultices, tinctures and smoke cleansing, and even dried and smoked in little clay pipes. A large number of sweat houses, almost three hundred, have been discovered in Ireland, with close to one hundred listed in Leitrim alone. They are thought to have been used to relieve a number of ailments. These little domed stone buildings would have a fire lit in the centre with turf or wood. The central chimney and doorway would be blocked for the fire to burn and heat the stone structure. The ashes were raked out and the patient would crawl through the little doorway and stay till they could sweat no more. These were all located next to water, rivers and lakes so that the patient could then submerge themselves in the cooling waters.

Nowadays we no longer need to sweat it out but we can still make use of smoke. Traditionally, native plants like juniper would be burned; sometimes a single twig would be lit, or dried herbs scattered on a fire. Native Americans have a very rich culture of smudging, a ceremony of burning sacred herbs, particularly white sage, cedar and sweetgrass. The plants and herbs used vary greatly from tribe to tribe and depend on the practitioners' specific rituals and beliefs. What some tribes choose to burn may be considered taboo for burning by others. Part of the ritual is planting, picking and bundling the herbs with your own hands and energy. It's just not the same buying a smudge stick online or in a shop.

All sage has powerful antibacterial, antioxidant and anti-inflammatory qualities. You can use purple or green sage from your own garden. Lavender, rose and rosemary also bring their own qualities, making these bundles look so beautiful and smell amazing.

Method

1 Using the sage as a base for each bundle, lay the lavender and rosemary on top.
2 Tie the end together with the twine, then top with some rose petals. Wrap the twine tightly around the bundle, holding everything in place.
3 When you're ready to use the bundle, crack open any doors and windows. Set your intentions and try to be in the moment; the whole process is very mindful.
4 Use a heatproof bowl or shell to hold your herb bundle.
5 Light the end until it starts to smoke. Let it burn for a few seconds – the flame should go out itself.
6 You can then carry the smoking bundle, with its bowl to catch ash, through the house to clear your space. Use both hands to waft the smoke towards you and wash away any negative energy.

Lilly's tips

▶ You can pick these herbs fresh, then hang them upside down to dry them, securing a paper bag under the roses to catch the petals. I find the bundles store better when formed with dry herbs.

Shell wall hanging

What you'll need:

Seashells
Small hammer
Twine or string
Scissors
Superglue
One stick to hang the shells from

A bit of wild crafting here for the month that's in it! A mix of twine and found shells, this hanging is a memory from the last of the summer beach days as we head into autumn. We stayed at the lovely Coulagh Bay Cottages on the Beara Peninsula in West Cork last summer, and there were lots of little shell crafts and wall hangings that have inspired this one. We always made crafts from shells when we were children, stacking them on top of one another to make little mice, trees and mermaids. My own children love the water so much, they could spend hours at the beach swimming and diving with their cousins. Wetsuits or not, they spend hours swimming and then dig moats, sandcastles and trenches along the sandy beaches. Once they're cosy and dressed, we barbecue sausages and everyone has hotdogs followed by toasted marshmallows. It's an August tradition that we always do for weeks before they head back to school, arriving home just as the sun settles in the horizon. This is a lovely project to do with those shells that end up coming home in buckets and bags.

Method

1 Plan out your design first before beginning. Try to make it symmetrical or do your own design.
2 Tap the top of each shell with a small hammer to create a hole to thread the twine through.
3 Thread the shells onto the string and tie a knot after each one is added. Glue any shells that won't stay in place the way you want.
4 Tie each string of shells onto the stick. Tie some twine to the stick to hang it.

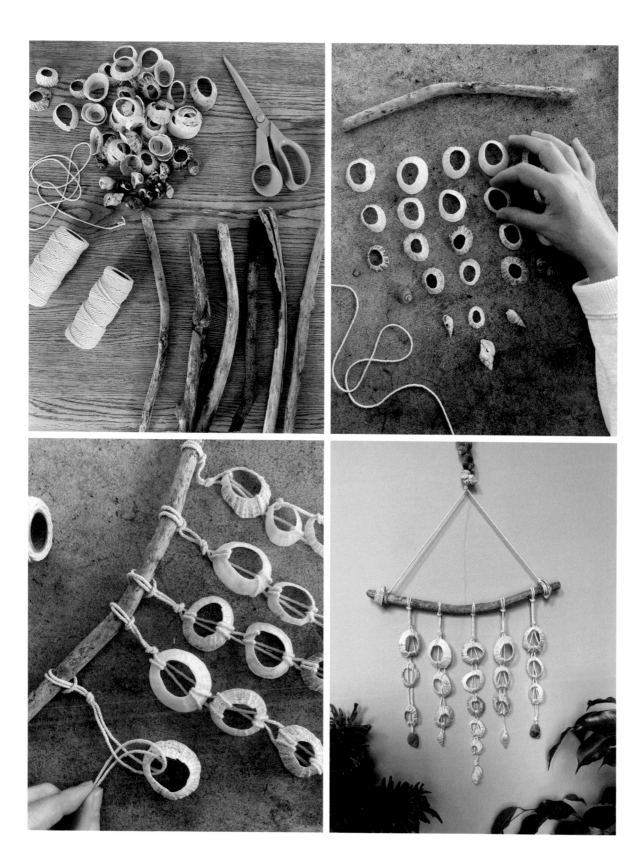

Dried hydrangeas

What you'll need:

Healthy hydrangeas
Sharp garden shears or pruners
Vases or jugs to dry the
hydrangeas in

Hydrangeas are having a moment, aren't they? My granny was immensely proud of her hydrangeas. She moved from her old farmhouse in the 1970s and built a new, modern house complete with rows of bright hydrangeas alongside the driveway and thick, dark green conifer hedging. I always remember how much she loved the pink and blue flowers. She would never pick them and bring them indoors, but she would set up her deck chair outside alongside them, and sit in the sun with her legs outstretched as all the colourful fluffy flowers also gazed south towards the sun. The hydrangeas were always the first things we commented on when we wandered up the driveway, admiring them aloud as we drew closer to the house. My favourites in my own garden are Runaway Bride – it's the most floriferous, producing six times more flowers than the average hydrangea. It has beautiful white flowers with such a classic look. I also adore the conical Limelight variety and Blushing Bride: its white flowers mature to a light pink or light blue, depending on soil pH. I'm also totally amazed by the growth of my climbing hydrangea. It clings to the wall like ivy and is such a lovely plant. Happily, most hydrangeas dry well, so can be enjoyed indoors all year round. There are so many ways to use dried flowers: single stems are lovely in bud vases. Mix full bunches or add them to wreaths and garlands. A wreath made entirely of dried hydrangeas is really beautiful. They'll last for years and you can dust them with a blast of cold air from a hairdryer.

Method

1 It may seem to make sense to pick hydrangeas at full bloom but it's better to let them dry a little on the plant first. Let nature begin the gentle process for you. Once the petals begin to feel papery and the colour begins to change, it's time to pick them.

2 Use sharp shears or pruners to cut the stems at an angle. It's best to cut them in the morning after the dew has dried from the petals. Pick the best, healthiest flowers and remove all the leaves

3 There are two easy ways to dry these flowers at home: the wet and the dry method. To follow the former, fill the vases and jugs with about 8cm of water and space the flowers out evenly, giving enough room for air to circulate around them. The water will evaporate slowly as the flowers dry. I find this wet method preserves the colour a little better and gives a slower drying time overall.

4 To follow the dry method, simply place the flowers in vases around your home and leave them to dry out naturally themselves.

5 Keep the flowers out of direct sunlight as they dry. They're ready for use in about two weeks, when the stems snap easily.

Lilly's tips

▶ Leave any old flowers you don't cut in place through the winter to protect the plant. It might be tempting to prune them but wait till new shoots start to emerge in spring.

Pickled vegetables

What you'll need:

1 litre vinegar (white, apple
    cider, etc.)
1 litre water
2 tbsp sugar
4–5 tbsp salt
**Vegetables and flavourings
    of your choice**
Glass jars

**Makes 6 × 500ml jars (halve the
recipe for a smaller batch)**

This is one of my favourite ways to preserve vegetables. It's an ideal way to avoid food waste in your own kitchen while doing a little bit of meal prep too! These pickles are so handy to have in the fridge. Quick pickles are fun and easy to make, with so many different flavour possibilities – plus they're delicious. I've listed some of my very favourite flavour combinations on the next page. They keep in the fridge for up to two months. So if you've got half a cucumber just pickle it! Pop leftover sliced onion into that jar too, and you've got a lovely addition to sandwiches and a topping for curries or salads. You can use any vinegar except balsamic and the syrupy darker ones. I buy big 5-litre bottles of Irish apple cider vinegar from Future Orchard in Cork.

Lilly's favourite flavourings

Cherry tomatoes, jalapeños, chopped coriander stalks, lime peel, red onion

Cauliflower, yellow pepper, red onion, ground turmeric, garam masala, bay leaves, coriander seeds, mustard seeds

Carrots, thyme, fennel seeds

Cucumber, red onion, dill

Red onion, orange peel, allspice berries, and a blackcurrant hibiscus tea bag steeped in the vinegar for flavour & colour

Radish and ginger

Method

1 Simply heat the water and vinegar in a pan, then add the sugar and salt. Heat till both are dissolved, then set aside for 10 minutes before using.
2 Chop the vegetables into the sizes you want. Place spices and herbs in each clean jar and top with veg, leaving about 1cm space at the top. Pour over the warm vinegar mixture. Seal with a lid. Leave to cool at room temperature, then place in the fridge.
3 The pickles taste best after 48 hours and will last for up to 2 months. Once the vegetables have been eaten the pickling juice can be reused! Just add more vegetables or use in salad dressings.

Painted terracotta pots

What you'll need:

Terracotta pot
A pencil
Acrylic or spray paints
Paintbrushes
Masking tape
Letter stamps and ink pad, or
   permanent markers
Clear varnish, for outdoor use

I really love my herb bed and have lots of different varieties of mint and thyme. Lemon balm and mint are very easy to plant, so I always give slips to my friends so they can grow them at home too. Simply pick a stem of mint or lemon balm and sit it in a cup of water. After a week or so, shoots will begin to appear. You can then plant this slip in compost in a pot. I can never grow basil outdoors, so I usually have a pot in the kitchen by the window.

This project is a great way to reuse old, cracked pots to grow more herbs. Decorate them and sit a plastic pot inside. We love to decorate the pots with leftover paints – it's a lovely outdoor project that everyone can take part in. It's also a great way to learn herb varieties, so use simple stampers or a permanent marker to write the names on the pots.

Method

1 Lightly draw your design onto the pot using the pencil.
2 Use the brush to paint on the design, or use masking tape to help mask off areas and use spray paint.
3 Leave to dry completely before adding your plant.
4 You can now keep your plant indoors or paint the pot with clear varnish and keep it outdoors.

The Harvest Moon

Moons of the year

January: Wolf Moon

February: Snow Moon

March: Worm Moon

April: Pink Moon

May: Flower Moon

June: Strawberry Moon

July: Buck Moon

August: Sturgeon Moon

September: Harvest Moon

October: Hunter's Moon

November: Beaver Moon

December: Cold Moon

The Harvest Moon appears around the time of the autumn equinox, when farmers tend to do their main crop harvesting. The light of the full moon enables the farmers to work late into the night bringing crops in from the fields. When I was little I could hear the hum of the tractors rattling along the road past our house and see their lights flooding the nearby fields late at night.

You can mark the Harvest Moon by doing some new moon rituals. All new moons mean a fresh start and the beginning of another 28-day cycle. Each month of the year has its own special full moon. Ancient cultures around the world have given these full moons names based on the behaviour of the animals, weather and plants that month. The Harvest Moon is the most widely known. These are the Native American names that are now commonly used for each new moon the world over.

New moon rituals

A new moon is the perfect time to question old habits, behaviours and beliefs as you search for new and inventive ways to make progress. These are great new moon rituals to check in with yourself and make yourself feel more grounded.

- Set intentions and manifest what it is you're aiming for. Write down your intentions and store them under a crystal. Choose an aligning crystal (rose quartz for love, amazonite for confidence, amethyst for balance, etc.). Check back on these intentions at the next full moon.
- Focus on your wellbeing. Release and wash away worries with a bath or shower.
- Set up your space by lighting a candle, arranging crystals and flowers.
- Meditate. Sit still and breathe deeply for 10 minutes or do a guided meditation. YouTube is an excellent resource for guided meditations, or use an app.
- Cleanse away stagnant air. Open windows in your house or use a smudge stick (see Herb bundles, page 176, for how to make your own).

Rosehip oil

What you'll need:

150g fresh rosehips
500ml almond, olive or jojoba oil
Slow cooker
Sieve
Cloth, such as a muslin
Dark glass bottle or jar

When I had my first baby, Liam, my sister Raedi gave me lots of lovely potions and lotions. One was a bottle of beautiful rosehip oil. For the first busy few months my only act of self-care was warming those golden drops in my hands and spreading them on my face before I collapsed into bed! By the time I had my third baby I realised just how important these rituals of self-care are. It's hard to run on empty. Now those babies help me to pick the rosehips and make this beautiful skin oil. Packed with antioxidants and fatty acids, rosehip oil is a natural and versatile moisturiser for your hair, nails and skin. Rosehip oil comes from the fruit of the roses, the rosehips. There are several types and all are safe to use on your skin. Only pick them on a dry day, from chemical-free rose bushes, and wear gloves to protect against thorns. I use a slow cooker here, but the oil can also be infused in the oven, in a heavy-based lidded pot, on as low a setting as possible for 8 hours.

Method

1 Remove any leaves, stems or thorns from the rosehips.
2 Combine the rosehips with the oil in a slow cooker. Stir to mix.
3 Place the lid on and set it to low for 8 hours. The oil will smell fragrant and be orange in colour when fully infused.
4 Strain the oil through a sieve lined with cloth and compost the rosehip solids.
5 Pour the oil into a dark glass jar or bottle. Store in the fridge for 6–8 months.

Scrunchies

What you'll need:

Fabric, 46cm × 12cm
Thread
Needle
Small bulldog clip
Hair band/bobble
Scissors

Growing up with six sisters meant that there were plenty of hair accessories in our house. I remember my mother washing and ironing our ribbons. For a solid two years in playschool I had two long plaits with ribbons at the end. Once the ribbons became tatty, we used them for Christmas decorations or for our dolls' hair. In Zimbabwe we discovered the world of scrunchies. One of my mother's friends had a sewing machine and used to create the most amazing ruffled scrunchies with fabric remnants. We loved having one in our hair and a matching one on our wrist. Now I make them with my own fabric scraps. Natural fibres like cotton, linen and especially silk, if you can find it, are great for scrunchies as they don't damage the hair. It's a great way to use any leftover fabric and gives my daughter and nieces a little pep in their step returning back to school in September. Having a matching scrunchie is a lovely way to make an outfit pop.

Method

1 Thread your needle.
2 Fold the fabric in half lengthwise, with the right/patterned side facing in, aligning the edges together. Use the bulldog clip to keep the fabric layers in place.
3 Place the hair bobble at one end, between the two layers of fabric.
4 Sew the long edges together using a running stitch, starting at the end and working your way around the band. For this and other simple sewing techniques, see my guide on page 324.
5 Turn the tube inside out. Fold the ends of the tube inside to conceal the raw edges and put one end of the tube inside the other. Sew the ends together using a slip stitch.

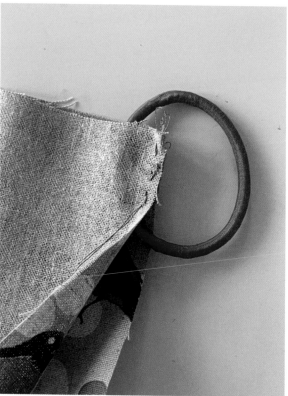
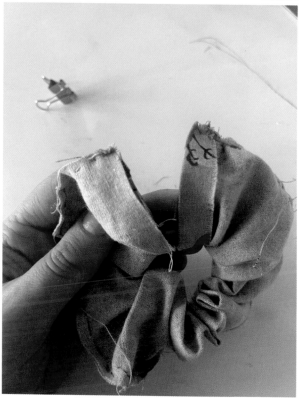
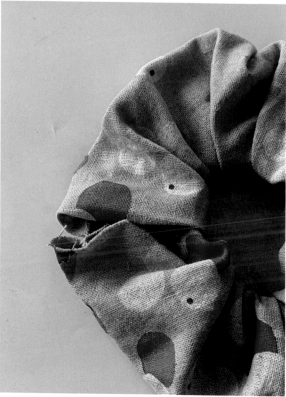

Homemade pizzas

For the quick sauce:

What you'll need:
1 × 400g tin chopped tomatoes
1 clove garlic
1 tsp dried herbs (oregano or basil)
1 tbsp chia seeds
½ tsp salt
½ tsp brown sugar
Black pepper

For the cooked tomato sauce:

What you'll need:
2 tbsp olive oil
1 onion, diced
½ stick celery, finely chopped
1 carrot, peeled and diced
2 cloves garlic, crushed
1 × 400g tin chopped tomatoes
½ tsp brown sugar
Salt & black pepper
2 tbsp fresh basil, oregano or
   marjoram

I love being able to rely on pizzas for an easy dinner after a busy day of school, swimming lessons or soccer. Once the lazy days of summer are over and school begins, so do the after-school activities, and some days we don't get home till dinnertime. Get one step ahead by prepping a big batch of this easy pizza dough. You can keep it in your fridge for a few days or pre-bake the bases like I do. This way all you need to do is add the sauce and your choice of topping, then pop in a hot oven for a few minutes while you rustle up a salad. I love this quick and easy no-cook tomato sauce that relies on chia seeds to thicken it. You can also make a more traditional tomato sauce with added vegetables as a way to boost the nutritional content even more.

For the pizza dough:

What you'll need:
800g plain flour, plus extra for
   dusting the work surface
2 × 7g sachets fast-action dried
   yeast (2 tsp)
2 tsp fine sea salt
2 tsp brown sugar
450ml lukewarm water
4 tbsp olive oil, plus a little extra

To complete the pizzas:

Toppings of choice: mozzarella,
   grated cheese, salami slices, etc.

Makes 4 large pizzas

Method

1 Preheat the oven to 220°C.
2 First, make the sauce. For the quick sauce, just blitz everything in a
   high-speed blender, such as a Nutribullet, till smooth. Set the sauce
   aside so the chia seeds can thicken it before you spread it on the
   bases.
3 If making the cooked sauce, pour 2 tbsp oil into a heavy-based
   medium-sized pan. Add the onion, celery and carrot. Sauté for a few
   minutes before adding the garlic. Cook for 2 minutes, stirring all the
   time so the garlic doesn't burn.
4 Add the chopped tomatoes and brown sugar. Season with salt and
   black pepper. Simmer till the vegetables are cooked, about 10 minutes.
   Remove from the heat and leave to cool slightly. Add the herbs to the
   pan and blitz everything till smooth with a handheld blender, or use a
   food processor. Set aside.
5 Now to make your dough! Place the flour, yeast, salt and sugar in a
   mixing bowl. Use a wooden spoon to mix. Make a well in the centre
   and pour in the lukewarm water and the olive oil. Bring together
   to form a dough. Knead for a minute on a floured work surface till
   smooth. Pour a little oil into the mixing bowl and place the dough in
   the bowl. Cover the bowl with a plate to allow the dough rest for five
   minutes.
6 Lightly dust a work surface with flour. Divide the dough into four balls,
   and roll each into a large oval shape. Drizzle a little olive oil on a tray
   for a crispy base or dust with flour for a softer base. Lay the dough on
   the tray. If eating these pizzas right away, spread on the sauce and
   toppings now before baking till golden, 10–12 minutes.
7 To parbake, just pop the plain pizza bases into the oven for 5–8
   minutes until lightly golden and puffed up in places. Then remove the
   pizza bases and leave to cool on a wire rack. You can then store the
   bases in the fridge till ready to cook, for up to 3 days. These prebaked
   pizzas will only take 5 minutes to cook in a very hot oven, 220°C.

Lilly's tips

▶ Prebaked pizza bases can be frozen too: just wrap them well, with a
   layer of greaseproof paper between each base, and store for up to 3
   months. Bake from frozen for 10–15 minutes.

Planting spring bulbs

What you'll need:

Bulbs such as daffodils, crocuses, hyacinths or tulips
Gloves (not essential but a great help)
A trowel
Pots and compost, if not planting directly into the soil

As we slowly accept that summer is no longer, we begin to notice the beauty in the wilting flowers, the changing colours of the leaves and the beautiful autumn light. Pink skies in the morning and the late September sun that warms like no other. When I first moved out of home, I missed not having flowers magically bloom in spring. I had never really thought about how those tulips and daffodils just appear! My parents' driveway was always lined with a frilly border of daffodils that seemed to have come out of nowhere. So now each autumn I plant spring bulbs too, layering various tulips in a lasagne style in terracotta pots, arranging bulbs by flower height in the borders and choosing colour schemes in pots so that I can place them where I need them.

Plant spring-flowering and hardy summer-flowering bulbs in autumn and fragile summer-flowering bulbs in early spring. Most hardy bulbs, including tulips and daffodils, prefer a warm, sunny site and good drainage. Use corks from wine bottles in the base of your pots; they're light and facilitate drainage. Pots are fantastic for creating bursts of colour and you can place them where you need them in the garden.

Method

1 Remove stones and weeds to prepare the soil before planting.
2 Bulbs should be planted 2–3 times the depth of the bulb. So if a bulb measures 4cm dig a hole that's 8cm–12cm deep.
3 Face the pointed end of the bulb upwards and the root end facing down.
4 Backfill the hole and compress the soil lightly; water it gently if it's a dry day.

Lilly's tips

When to plant:
▶ Bare root trees and shrubs: November to March, during their 'dormant season'
▶ Root ball plants, mature trees and shrubs: November to March, during their 'dormant season'
▶ Shrubs and trees in containers: April to October, and keep them watered well
▶ Perennials, grasses and ferns: November to March, during their 'dormant season', is best but in reality all year round is fine – just water and mulch well
▶ Daffodils, crocuses and hyacinths: September and October
▶ Tulips and crocuses: November

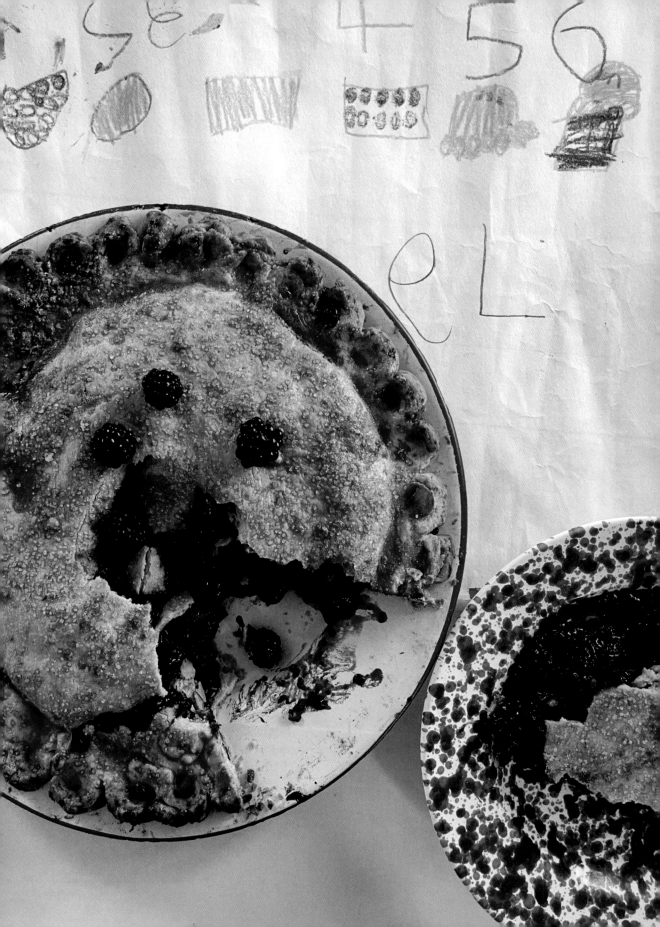

Apple and blackberry tart

For the pastry:

What you'll need:
150g cold butter, cubed
240g plain flour
20g icing sugar
1 egg

For the filling:

What you'll need:
1kg apples, peeled and diced
 (Bramley or eating apples)
2 handfuls of blackberries
50g soft brown sugar and extra for
 sprinkling on top
1 tsp cornflour

To finish:

What you'll need:
1 egg, whisked, for egg wash

Makes 1 tart

Late August into September is prime time to pick blackberries.

We had an absolutely gorgeous Doberman cross called Bo for eight years; we adored her and she was there to welcome each of our babies home from the hospital. Months later, they crawled towards her and learned to walk leaning on her. She was a true family pet. She really loved blackberries too, and would gingerly pick them from the lowest bushes, avoiding any thorns as she did. The boys would give her all of their pickings and we would wander home empty-handed but with a very happy pup.

When we were little, we always picked blackberries in my granddad's fields. One south-facing stretch of brambly ditch had the best, plumpest sun-soaked berries. We still go there today for them. We would always bring a big container each but never filled them. Our sticky, inked fingers tired from picking in between the briars. We'd resort to just playing in the fields and eating whatever we did pick, while my dad is a champion picker. He'd fill two huge Tupperware containers and bring them home for jam or blackberry tarts. My mother always made a mixed blackberry and apple tart that I love. It's such a lovely seasonal combination and makes the most of only a handful of blackberries – apple tart is always such a winner, but the blackberries transform it, while a little cornflour in the mix ensures the filling is thick and luscious. This tart is delicious with softly whipped cream or thick custard.

Method

1 Place the butter, flour and icing sugar in a food processor. Blitz till it forms fine breadcrumbs. Add the egg and mix again till a smooth dough forms. This can be done by hand too: just rub the butter into the flour mix, then mix the egg in with a round-bladed knife till it comes together.
2 Form a flat disc with the dough, wrap in greaseproof paper and place in the fridge to rest, for at least 10 minutes or as long as overnight.
3 Place the apples and half the blackberries into a small pan over a medium heat. You may need to add a splash of water depending on what type of apple is used. It doesn't need to be too wet. Simmer till all the fruit is soft and it begins to purée when stirred. Add the sugar to taste.
4 Set aside and leave to cool.
5 Preheat the oven to 180°C. I use a tart plate for this, an enamel or glass ovenproof shallow plate.
6 Roll the pastry out onto a floured surface and use your tart plate as a guide to cut two circles. Lay one disc of pastry onto the tart plate and pile the berry–apple mix in the middle.
7 Sift over the cornflour. This will thicken the fruit filling in the oven.
8 Scatter with the remaining blackberries, then brush the edges of the pastry with egg wash.
9 Lay the second disc of pastry over and crimp the edges to seal. Brush the tart with egg wash and scatter with brown sugar.
10 Cut two slits in the centre to allow steam to escape. Bake for 40–45 minutes till the pastry is golden and the fruit bubbling.

Lilly's tips

▶ When picking berries, avoid areas of heavy traffic pollution and dust. Leave some berries for wildlife! Only pick what you need. Pick on a dry day, not after heavy rain. Berries retain moisture, so will be more prone to mould if you pick them when they're soggy.

Toffee apples for Samhain and Halloween

What you'll need:

6 apples
Twigs or lollipop sticks (if you're
   using twigs, make sure to clean
   them well and dry them first)
550g sugar
300ml water
1 tsp vinegar
A tray lined with greaseproof paper
Sea salt for sprinkling

Makes 6

Apples are the most traditional food in Ireland for Halloween and Samhain. Traditionally all the crops would be harvested by now. It would be the end of the year's growth and no apple or blackberry was worth picking after this night. Cattle were brought down from the mountains and bonfires lit to ward off the darkness. In Celtic mythology apples are strongly associated with immortality and the otherworld (the land of deities and those who've passed on). They were given as treats, pressed to make cider and juice to fuel the festivities, baked to make desserts, and hung off door frames and plunged into water for games on Halloween night. All you need for apple bobbing is some apples in a basin or bowl of water, some stuck with coins. No hands are allowed when trying to retrieve the apples, so you must dunk your head right into the water and try to catch an apple with your mouth. It's great fun and so messy.

These toffee apples are a very pretty way to make apples look more appetising to those in search of sugar. Small red apples are best for this; the more tang and sour flavour they have the better, to counteract the crunchy caramel shell. If you don't want to make caramel, you can always decorate the apples with melted chocolate. Either way, they are a lovely way to celebrate Samhain and Halloween.

Method

1 Boil the kettle so you'll have hot water to clean the pan once you're done. Fill a large basin or sink with cold water for cooling the saucepan. Lay out everything else you need, as you'll have to work quickly once the caramel is ready.

2 Wash the apples well. Remove the stalks, then firmly spear each one through the centre with a twig or stick.

3 Heat the sugar, water and vinegar in a heavy-based pan until the sugar dissolves. Turn up the heat once dissolved completely, and let the mixture boil until it turns a caramel colour. This should take approximately 10 minutes, but watch it carefully so it doesn't get too dark.

4 Take off the heat and immediately sit the pan in cold water to stop it cooking.

5 Work quickly. Dip each apple into the caramel to coat it evenly, then place on the tray.

6 Sprinkle the top of each apple with a little salt.

7 These will last 2–3 hours before the caramel starts to soften.

Lilly's tips

▶ Add a tablespoon of pomegranate molasses to the caramel for a tart taste and deeper colour.

A herbal tonic for sore throats

What you'll need:

8 sage leaves, chopped
4 sprigs of thyme, chopped (leaves
   and stems)
4 thick slices of ginger
250ml apple cider vinegar
250ml raw honey
1 large jar

Makes 500ml

With the change in weather come the coughs, colds and sore throats. It's inevitable each year once school begins that various different maladies will make their way home. I love having a traditional herbal remedy, oxymel, at hand as a source of comfort for those sore throats. I stir it through warm water or just have a soothing spoonful. Essentially it's a honey–vinegar mix that can be infused with any herbs and spices you like. I'm focusing on sore throats here, so sage is instantly what comes to mind, along with thyme and ginger for warmth and to stimulate the immune system. You may have heard of fire cider: it's an apple cider vinegar and honey infusion with turmeric, ginger, horseradish and many more fiery, immune-boosting components. There are many different oxymels and it's great fun to experiment with them. I find them great as salad dressings too, with a little olive oil.

You can also use this oxymel as a soft drink by mixing it with soda water; that balance of sweet and sour is so refreshing.

Method

1 Fill the jar ¼ to ⅓ full with chopped herbs and sliced ginger.
2 Fill the jar to halfway with the vinegar, then top it up with honey. Fill the jar as full as you can. The less air space at the top the better, as you don't want the sage turning brown. Place the lid on and shake well. The vinegar will dissolve the honey over time. Leave to sit in a dark place for a month.
3 Once the 30 days are up, strain the liquid and discard the leaves and ginger. Pour the tonic into a jar with a lid and store in a cool cupboard (or the fridge) for 6 months or more.
4 Adults can take 1–2 tbsp three times a day or whenever they're feeling under the weather. I give one teaspoon at a time to my kids. It's sometimes a little acidic for their liking, so I stir it through warm water with a little more honey as a soothing drink. It's also great in salad dressings or drizzled over roast vegetables.

Lilly's tips

▶ Make a garlic and thyme oxymel by filling a jar ⅓ full with peeled garlic, then add equal parts vinegar and honey. Leave for 2–3 weeks at room temperature. The garlic is delicious and can be used as well as the honey mix.

Halloween treat box

What you'll need:

Empty toilet paper tubes
Black and white paint
Paint brushes
Paper or card, black if you have it
Scissors
Glue stick
Greaseproof paper
Sweets

This is a really great method for making a toilet roll tube into something useful! These little pillow boxes are handy for so many things. To sanitise toilet paper rolls, you can first collect them over a period of time, then preheat your oven to low (100°C will do) and position all the toilet rolls in the centre on the racks. Bake for 15 minutes to heat thoroughly and kill any lingering bacteria. Never leave the paper rolls unattended in the oven. There's a very slight risk of them burning at this low temperature, but it's still best to keep an eye on them. Leave to cool fully before painting. If you don't like the idea of using toilet paper rolls for this, any empty cardboard tube will work, from wrapping paper to kitchen towels or tinfoil. Just cut it down to size.

I've made bats here for a Halloween theme, but with the pillow shape these make excellent witches' cats too. Add some bunny ears for a very cute Easter treat box or make little snowmen for Christmas. There are so many possibilities and it's a great craft for all ages to get involved with.

Method

1 Start by painting the paper rolls black. Paint the paper or card too if it's not black already.
2 Once dry, flatten a toilet paper roll. Press the creases at either side flat. Let the tube pop back up slightly, then push the top of the tube down towards the middle, so it creates a rounded fold. Then push the other side the same way to close off one end of the tube.
3 Repeat with the other end. Glue one end closed; the other end can be the opening.
4 Cut two bat wings from the paper or card. Glue these onto the back of the box. Add eyes and a mouth to make your bat face.
5 Wrap some sweets in greaseproof paper and pop them into the box. Seal with a little bit of glue or double-sided tape. Repeat with the remaining rolls.

Carving pumpkins

What you'll need:

**Pumpkin – choose large, tall
  pumpkins with a wide surface area**
A sharp serrated knife
**Spoons – I find soup spoons
  work well**
Paper for planning your design
**A marker or pen for drawing on your
  design**
**Smaller sharp serrated knives for
  carving**
A nightlight, candle or LED light

Originally here in Ireland we carved turnips or sugar beet. It's so difficult to do! When Irish immigrants settled in America there were no turnips to be found, but they did have plenty of pumpkins come Halloween time. The large orange pumpkins are much softer and easier to carve. Hence the tradition of carving Jack O'Lanterns from pumpkins.

Each year we fill our house with pumpkins of all types and sizes. I always display them around the house and outside on the doorstep all month. I like it when they are not carved because you can eat them more easily – slice them into wedges or in half and roast them with a little chilli oil. Delicious with crumbled feta!

It's best to wait to carve them till the last minute as they'll quickly begin to rot, especially if you're placing a candle inside. The mixture of warmth and gourd is never a sweet-smelling one! After carving your pumpkin, brush the inside of it with a vinegar solution to dampen down any bacteria from forming. It'll last twice as long.

I keep a collection of smaller round gourds dotted around the house, on the mantelpiece and on the table. I keep the larger ones for carving. Choose wisely when at the farmers' market or shop!

Method

1 Slice the top off your pumpkin carefully using a serrated knife and set aside.
2 Hollow out the inside of the pumpkin and thin the shell. Keep as much of the pumpkin flesh as you can for making soup. Keep the seeds to wash and dry well for planting more pumpkins.
3 Draw your design on paper first. Think outside the box – it can be anything you like.
4 Draw the design on the pumpkin using a marker.
5 Use a small, serrated knife to cut out the design. Always cut away from yourself in case the knife slips.
6 Be patient and take your time when carving. Don't try to make it perfect: each one is unique.
7 Add a candle or small LED light. The pumpkins always look better lit up.

Apple butter

What you'll need:

1.5kg apples, peeled, quartered and
  cored. Any Irish apples will be
  ideal for this
Zest and juice of ½ lemon
300g sugar
2 tsp cinnamon
½ tsp ground cloves
1 tbsp molasses (optional)

Makes 4–6 jam jars

My mother once cut out an article for me from a magazine all about the traditional black butter-making that takes place in Jersey. Black butter is a rich conserve of apples, cider and spices. Traditionally Black Butter Nights were held after apple harvest each year. It was a really communal affair that I just love the sound of. Huge barrels of cider, apples, spices and sugar were simmered and stirred together over an open fire for 24 hours. Singing, dancing, chatting and storytelling all followed into the early hours of the morning.

If you're lucky enough to have access to plenty of homegrown Irish apples this time of year, then make the most of it. Locally grown apples can be bought cheaply by the bagful at farmers' markets. Every year, I make huge batches of apple butter: a thick apple paste spiced with cinnamon and sweetened with a little sugar. Spread it over pancakes or serve with scones in place of jam. It's also amazing stirred into hot cider for a perfectly spiced autumnal tipple.

Method

1 Place the quartered apples in a large pot with the lemon juice. Bring to the boil and reduce to a simmer for 20 minutes or until the apples are soft. Cooking apples will be wetter and break down faster; firmer eating apples may need some water to encourage them to break down. If the base of the pot is not covered in some liquid after a few minutes of cooking, add 100ml of water.

2 Work the apple mixture through a food mill or sieve and into a large bowl. You can also use a stick blender. Add the sugar, spices, lemon zest and molasses.

3 Cook, uncovered, in a wide, shallow pan, stirring occasionally to make sure none of the mixture sticks to the bottom. Cook this way for 1–2 hours, until the mixture has thickened.

4 You can then place the apple butter into sterilised jars, freeze, or use immediately. Unopened jars will keep for 6 months. Once opened, store in the fridge for up to 1 month.

Lilly's tips

▶ To make in the slow cooker, add all ingredients to the slow cooker, and then cook on high for 4 hours, stirring every hour. Blitz till smooth.

Apple scrap vinegar

What you'll need:

The peels and cores from about
  6 apples, or a similar volume of
  sliced-up whole apples
1 tbsp sugar
A 500ml jar
1 fabric napkin (muslin, cotton or
  linen)
1 elastic band
Bottles for storage

Makes 500ml

I first made this about eight years ago when we had our own apples growing in the garden. It felt like such a waste not to use every last scrap of this beautiful fruit, having seen it grow from bud to blossom and then rosy-cheeked apple. Then I discovered that the skins of those organic apples had such life in them: once fermented in sugar water, they bubbled and changed into a gorgeous vinegar. This is a lovely light vinegar that's great for salad dressings or marinades.

There are so many different fruit scrap vinegars you can make, from pineapple to pear.

Of course, if you don't have scraps, you can use whole apples instead!

Method

1 Place all the apple scraps in the jar and add the sugar. Top up with cooled boiled water. The peels need to stay submerged under the surface.
2 No need for a lid. Place the fabric napkin over the mouth of the jar. Use the elastic band to hold it in place.
3 Leave the mix to ferment for 1–2 weeks, stirring and checking every day to ensure the apple scraps are still submerged.
4 Strain and compost the scraps. The vinegar will now smell like a mild cider. Keep the vinegar in a jar on the countertop, covered with a cloth, for another 2–4 weeks until it develops its acidic tang. By now the sugar should be well spent and fermentation should be over. If it's still quite bubbly and carbonated, then keep in the jar. Once it's flat and acidic it can be bottled safely.
5 Transfer the vinegar into bottes and seal. If you do spot any bubbles forming, you can slowly open the bottles and 'burp' them to release the pressure.

Lilly's tips

▶ Try flavouring your vinegar once strained: you can use chives, raspberries, wild garlic flowers and more. There are lots of ideas for flavouring your vinegar on page 111.

Barmbrack/báirín breac

What you'll need:

300ml hot tea (made with 2 normal
    teabags and 1 earl grey/cinnamon
    and liquorice/spiced chai, etc.)
180g sultanas
180g raisins
100g chopped dried dates
1 egg
1–2 tbsp orange juice
150g brown sugar
225g self-raising flour
2 tsp mixed spice
2 tbsp honey, to glaze
Trinkets (optional), wrapped well in
    baking paper!

Makes 1 barmbrack

This recipe has been handed down to me by my mother. It's her tea brack but I've tweaked it a little. No Halloween spread is complete without a barmbrack. It's a spooky fortune-telling loaf that also tastes delicious with butter and a hot cup of tea. Such a winning combination! My kids love to bake this with me each year. The trinkets sunk into the batter symbolise what will happen in your future, so make sure to include a few for fun. I always add the ring and coin, wrapped in baking paper, but the others are optional! It's rare to find most of these fortune-telling tokens in shop-bought barmbracks, as they're choking hazards, so make sure you wrap them up well and inform everyone they're there. I once found a rag in a brownie that I was eating in a café in Edinburgh. The prophecy there was that I would never go to that café again!

Fortune-telling trinkets

The ring: impending marriage, but only if you're single

The coin: predicts wealth and fortune

The rag: bad luck and poverty, sorry!

The stick: an unhappy marriage

The pea: you won't be getting married anytime soon

The medal: you'll join a religious order

Method

1. The day before you bake, make the tea and leave to stand for 15 minutes.
2. Place the sultanas, raisins and chopped dates into a bowl. Remove the tea bags from the pot and pour the hot tea over the fruit. Cover and leave overnight to soak.
3. The next day preheat the oven to 180°C. Line a 23cm × 12cm loaf tin with baking parchment.
4. Whisk the egg. Add to the fruit mix along with the orange juice, sugar, flour and mixed spice. Mix well with a wooden spoon.
5. Spoon into the prepared tin and push any wrapped trinkets halfway down into the batter. Bake for 1½ hours or until a skewer comes out clean.
6. Turn out onto a wire rack and, while still quite warm, brush the top with the honey.

Winter
Samhain

November, December, January

1 November is the Celtic festival of Samhain and also the Feast of All Saints. Samhain is considered to be the earliest incarnation of Halloween that we have here in Ireland – although they are two separate festivals. Samhain is a Gaelic festival marking the end of the harvest season and beginning of winter or the 'darker half' of the year. It is held on 1 November, but with celebrations beginning on the evening of 31 October, since the Celtic day began and ended at sunset. The Hindu festival Diwali, also known as the Festival of Lights, occurs about the same time. Diwali marks the Hindu new year just as Samhain marks the Celtic new year. Both mark this time with lights, candles and fire.

At Samhain, it's believed that the spirits of those who have died in the previous year pass on to the next world. It's like an Irish version of Día de los Muertos, but without the amazing Mexican face paints and gorgeous altars. I really love the idea of little altars, though. One of my children made one this year, and found it a really lovely, cathartic thing to do to remember our loved ones. One of my favourite December traditions growing up was to collect moss for the crib. We would go to a nearby woodland and look for the softest mossy patches, then lift off tufts of bright green moss, shaking off the little bugs that were snuggled into it. We had a very simple crib with carved wooden figures of Mary, Joseph and Jesus that my parents bought in Zimbabwe when we were little. I still love seeing it each year and based my gingerbread version on that. We spent two Christmases in Africa, running around outside in our summer dresses. The Christmas we moved home to Ireland, in 1993, it snowed like magic and we discovered selection boxes and chocolate coins. Festive food has always been such a delight to me. Everything is richer, more abundant, and flavours are exaggerated. These are not just toasted nuts, they're maple-kissed rosemary and cayenne pepper toasted nuts! There are so many amazing Christmas traditions. I've included a handful of my ultimate favourites, but really there's an entire book worth of things to make and do for Christmas!

I just adore the festive season so I always need something to look forward to in the new year, once the rush of Christmas is over. My granddad used to always plant hyacinth bulbs in winter. This was a tradition he got from his own grandmother – the Victorians loved hyacinths and revered them for their lingering, sweet fragrance. He would bury the bulbs in a pot and then place them under his bed in late autumn. Once green shoots appeared he would bring them into the light. Like me, he just adored Christmas and faded into a glum shadow of himself by January once all the fun was over. I think these hyacinths brought beauty, hope and an intoxicating smell into his world that reminded him of brighter days ahead. They always remind me so much of him.

The new year is the perfect time for a fresh start, setting out intentions for the coming months. Manifesting and making plans happen. It's a time of hope and I have some lovely projects to make that happen, from making your own kombucha to ensure good health to making your own gorgeous calendar and journals. Winter is a magical time when we see out the old year and welcome in the new, with plenty of enjoyable projects in between.

Leaf wreath

What you'll need:

Dried leaves in different sizes and
   colours
Twine or string
Scissors
1 wreath base
Ribbon bow (optional)

Going for a walk and immersing yourself in nature is a really nice way to celebrate Samhain as it's all about the circle of life, respecting and appreciating what's around us. Create a Samhain centrepiece at your dinner table with pinecones, leaves and chestnuts. Or collect leaves and make a wreath like I have here. The colours in nature this time of year are so beautiful.

Instead of a roaring bonfire on top of a hill, why not light a few candles? Let their warming lights flicker in your home.

Make a memory table honouring loved ones who have passed away. Decorate it with leaves, drawings, objects from nature or things that remind you of that person. On Samhain, light a candle and think of them with love.

I do love a wreath for every season and this wreath of colourful autumn leaves is really beautiful. I've used a shop-bought base here and attached my leaves. These bases are widely available and usually cost less than five euro in crafts or home stores. The beauty is that they can be reused year after year. Simply strip the leaves off and start all over again. It's really lovely to have a piece of the outside world inside your house this time of year and it helps to make you feel more connected to the seasons.

Method

1 Group all of the leaves into similar colours or varieties. I like doing it by colour.
2 Make little bunches of 3–4 leaves and tie them together with the string, starting with the larger leaves first.
3 Layer the bunches of leaves on your base, tying them as you go.
4 You can work your way around the entire wreath or just do a burst of leaves at one side.
5 You can add a bow or keep it simple, making the leaves the focus of the wreath and acknowledging the season.

Facial steam

What you'll need:

Hair tie
Cleanser
A large bowl
**Herbs (camomile is good for
inflammation and dermatitis,
rosemary is great for oily skin)**
**Essential oils (optional; lavender is
relaxing and good for dry skin,
geranium tightens and tones, and
use eucalyptus for acne or if you're
congested)**
A large towel
Moisturiser or serum

Facial steams cleanse, nourish and feel so luxurious. The steam opens your pores and helps loosen any dirt for a deeper cleanse. It promotes circulation, which is so important at this time of year. The boost of blood flow nourishes your skin and delivers oxygen, giving you a natural, healthy glow. The increased blood flow also promotes collagen and elastin production, resulting in firmer, younger-looking skin. The steam increases your skin's permeability and helps your skin absorb skin care products, so it's ideal to use a good face cream or oil straight after.

Besides all this, it's so soothing. The feeling of warm steam on your face is so relaxing, especially if you add herbs or essential oils. It really helps with sinus congestion and headaches; adding certain essential oils can boost the effect. You can make your own botanical facial steam blend in a jar with a mix of dried rose petals, camomile and lavender. Such a nice gift idea! You can also benefit from steaming with herbal tea, such as green or white tea. And all this can be done at home with items you already have!

Method

1 Tie back your hair and cleanse your face and neck; ideally, gently exfoliate now too.
2 Pour an entire kettle of freshly boiled water into your bowl.
3 Add a handful of herbs and stir. Add a few drops of essential oils if using.
4 Sit facing the bowl and drape the towel over your head and the bowl. Hold your face 15–25cm above the water, whatever feels comfortable for you.
5 Raise your head a little if it gets too warm, or lift up a corner of the towel to cool off.
6 Keep your eyes closed as it's more comfortable and will prevent irritation.
7 Steam your face for 5–10 minutes.
8 Rinse your face with lukewarm water and gently pat dry. Apply a moisturiser or serum. Now's the perfect time to use those extra-nourishing creams and oils. You can gently massage your face with your fingertips for added benefits. I really love gua sha and practise at home with lovely facial oils. Gua sha stones are widely available and a great investment.

Wine cork trivet

What you'll need:

A collection of wine corks
A small pan
A serrated knife
Felt or heavy cardboard for backing
  the corks
Superglue

I'm a big fan of natural wines. I spent a few years studying wine and sitting the WSET (Wine & Spirit Education Trust) exams, but there was very little included on the wild wines that I love. It felt a bit like being back in school. I wanted to know more about the Georgian wines fermented underground in large clay pots called Qvevris, biodynamic wines made from multiple grape varieties where dogs and donkeys roam the vineyards. I love the naturally wild fermented wines, the characterful skin-contact wines and the bubbling pét-nats. All of these wines are made by smaller producers, families who have been making wine for generations or new winemakers trying something exciting. Popping the cork on one of these bottles and tasting the wine helps to tell these families' stories and supports them. I keep any corks from notable bottles to help me remember which ones we loved. Depending on the size of your cork collection, you can make bath mats, cork notice boards or coasters. This cute little trivet is perfect for placing under a hot dish or tea pot to protect your table. Fun and functional!

Method

1 For this project we have to cut the wine corks in half. Boil some water in a pan with the corks and simmer them for 10 minutes. This will clean them well and will make them easier to cut.

2 Once boiled, cut the corks on a wooden chopping board or other non-slip surface. Be careful! Use the serrated knife to cut the corks in half lengthways. Set aside and leave to dry before moving on to the next step.

3 Arrange your corks in whatever pattern you like. I've used a cross-hatch pattern for strength, and it looks nice too.

4 Once in place, measure and cut a piece of felt to be the bottom of the trivet. You will be gluing all the corks to this.

5 Place the felt square on a piece of card, to protect your work surface from glue. One by one, apply superglue to the cut side of each cork. Starting in the far left corner of your felt, press the cork down firmly right at the edge. Continue to build your trivet, copying the pattern you had laid out.

6 Once all the corks are in place, you can add a little extra glue around the joints to make sure they stay in place.

7 Leave to dry completely before neatly trimming away any visible pieces of felt.

Felt cup cosy

What you'll need:

Cups
Felt
Scissors
Pins
Embroidery thread
Embroidery needle

I always have my KeepCup with me, at my desk or in the car. It's either full of boiling water or tea, or I'm hoping to swing into my local coffee shop for a hot refill. It does look a bit battered after years of use, so this cup cosy is a nice way to give it a revamp. I love ceramic cups too, and really love finding new Irish ceramicists. There's something so tactile about clay – it holds the heat beautifully and knowing it's been handmade is so special.

These cup cosies are also perfect during the summer when I have freezing smoothies in the cups! They're also ideal for popping around a cup so small hands can get a better grip.

These are nice samplers for practising your embroidery. Felt is very forgiving and so easy to work with. Every little stitch you make will enhance your cosies and make them look even more unique. Try French knots, backstitching, blanket stitch and little x's. See page 325 for a basic guide to decorative stitches. This is also the perfect project to use up felt remnants and those odd pieces of embroidery thread.

These will really make your next flat white something special!

Method

1 Each cup is different, so start by cutting a strip of felt 7.5cm × 23cm. Wrap this around your cup and pin in place to gauge the size you will need. Trim off a small amount of felt at an angle to adjust it to the shape of your cup.

2 You can freehand your embroidery or draw designs on first, using tailor's chalk or a Sharpie in a similar colour to your felt. Choose your threads and get stitching (see page 324 for my guide to sewing and embroidery). Keep in mind where your designs will show up once the cosy is slipped over the coffee cup.

3 Finish by carrying the embroidery thread to the edge and stitching the ends together using a whip stitch, pinning the seam to hold everything in place while you sew. A whip stitch is a very basic stitch that involves poking the needle through two layers of fabric at an angle to finish an edge and join two pieces.

4 If your cosy is snug at first, that's fine, because the felt stretches a little as you use it. Now you can make lots more as gifts or to keep in your car for when you get a hot takeaway coffee.

Digestive biscuits

What you'll need:

250g plain flour
110g wholemeal flour
100g light brown sugar (coconut
    sugar works here too)
½ tsp bread soda
½ tsp baking powder
230g cold salted butter, cubed
110ml buttermilk

Makes 24

I just had to include one of my favourite biscuit recipes here. This time of year is all about cups of tea, hot chocolate and the oven humming with freshly baked goods. Rainy days are for baking, when recipes like this come into their own. I really love the versatility of these digestive biscuits. They're fantastic on their own, with just the right amount of salty sweetness, nicely balanced with the toasty wholemeal flour. I sometimes top them with melted dark or milk chocolate and a few flakes of sea salt. Truly decadent. Or I use them as a base for cheesecakes. They're also the ideal biscuit for making s'mores. A batch of these biscuits in a tin with squares of chocolate and marshmallows makes a really lovely gift to bring to your next family gathering.

Method

1 Place everything except the buttermilk in the bowl of a food processor. Blitz until it's a sandy consistency.
2 Add the buttermilk and blitz to a dough.
3 Turn out onto a work surface and smooth into a log shape. Wrap in baking paper and place in the fridge.
4 Preheat oven to 180°C.
5 Once the dough is cold, slice into 1cm-thick rounds and place on a baking sheet. Bake the biscuits for 8–10 mins, till the bases are golden.

Lilly's tips

▶ Once cooled, try spreading a teaspoon of melted chocolate on each biscuit and adding a sprinkle of sea salt.

Hot water bottle cover

What you'll need:

Newspaper
A hot water bottle
A black marker
Scissors
Pins
An old jumper or top with a nice
    pattern or fabric – natural fibres
    like wool or cotton work best
Thread
A needle
Ribbon to tie the top

So yes, it's getting pretty freezing out right about now! I'm a big fan of hot water bottles. I actually don't like the house being too warm, so I don't put on the heating that often, but rather focus on pulling on a cardigan or a pair of warmer socks. It's more environmentally friendly too!

I love hot water bottles. There's nothing nicer than climbing into bed to find that it's already warm and cosy. Hot water bottle covers make a really nice gift, especially this homemade version. Whenever I do a wardrobe clear-out I like to keep any damaged or worn clothes that I think can be reused. Nice fabrics are perfect for making hot water bottle covers. My kids love having one in their beds on cold nights or bringing one on a car journey. I usually tuck one into my husband's car when he's going for a winter swim. He always says he doesn't need it but comes back home hugging it! They're also great to have in the house for anyone with cramps, sore tummies or head colds. Gifting someone this pretty hot water bottle cover is sure to warm their hearts.

Method

1 Spread the newspaper on a table. Lay the water bottle on top and draw around it to make a rough shape.
2 Draw a 5cm border around that shape, then cut out along this border. Pin the paper to your fabric and cut out two copies of the shape.
3 Place the fabric pieces together inside out. Sew around the bottom and two sides of the outline, 1.5cm in from the edge of the fabric (see page 324 for my simple guide to sewing).
4 Turn the bag right way round and insert the hot water bottle. Tie the top with a ribbon.

Lilly's tips

▶ You can use this method to make a tea cosy, too. Just draw out a semi-circle on two pieces of fabric, making it big enough to fit over your teapot, and get sewing!

Gingerbread nativity scene

For the dough:

What you'll need:
170g butter, soft
250g light brown sugar
2 eggs
340g molasses, or alternatively agave syrup, honey or treacle
650g plain flour
½ tsp baking powder
2 tbsp ground ginger
2 tbsp mixed spice
1 tsp cinnamon
½ tsp salt
Greaseproof paper, pencil and scissors for making the templates
Sharp knife

For assembling and decorating:

What you'll need:
350g instant royal icing powder
5 tbsp water
Sweets such as gum drops, jelly beans, peppermint candy canes, dragées and marshmallows
Edible cake decorations like chocolate vermicelli or sprinkles
Granulated sugar for decorating the snow
A large cake board or similar
Piping bag fitted with a small plain nozzle
Small bowls or teacups for mixing small quantities of icing
Toothpicks

Makes enough dough for 1 stable, 1 crib, 3 characters and up to 20 tree decorations depending on size

Winter solstice is 21 December, the shortest day and longest night of the year, when the sun is lowest in the sky. The Irish for winter solstice, *an grianstad*, literally translates as 'the sun stop'. In secondary school we visited the Newgrange monument, the 5,200-year-old Neolithic passage tomb in the Boyne Valley, Co. Meath. It's surrounded by 97 large kerbstones, some engraved with swirling megalithic art. At sunrise, on this shortest day, direct sunlight creeps through the roof box and illuminates the chamber. It really is phenomenal and incredible that they were able to create such an accurate astronomical feature in those times.

A few short days after the winter solstice, our world is lit with twinkling lights as Christmas falls on 25 December. Christmas is the highlight of winter in our home. I've always loved this time of year, even before we had our children and got to experience it through their eyes. My eldest was born the night I hauled a Christmas tree from the boot of my Jeep. He's been a festive baby ever since, and we always have the tree up for his birthday at the start of December.

This gingerbread nativity is another tradition we still do. I first made one over a decade ago and now I bake one each year. Some are gaudy and bright, others simpler and more modern. Decorate it however you like; it's simpler than a full-blown gingerbread house and a lovely way to mark the occasion, with a sweet baby Jesus taking centre stage.

Method

1 Cream the butter and sugar together until light and fluffy. Add the eggs one at a time, beating well after each addition. Pour in the molasses and mix well.

2 Sieve the flour, baking powder, spices and salt into a separate bowl. Add half the sieved flour mixture to the molasses mixture. Once combined, add the remaining flour and mix until it becomes a smooth dough. Halve the dough and flatten into two discs. Wrap with cling film and place in the fridge to firm up for an hour or overnight.

3 Preheat the oven to 180°C.

4 Prepare the templates by tracing the characters and stable pieces onto greaseproof paper and then cutting around them. Or use ready-made biscuit cutters.

5 Roll out half the dough between two large baking tray-sized sheets of greaseproof paper, as it can be sticky to work with. Once flattened, place in the freezer, still on the sheet of greaseproof paper, for 10 minutes. Repeat with the rest of the dough.

6 Place the templates on the cold dough and cut around them using a small, sharp knife. Remove all the excess dough. You can use the leftover dough to make extra biscuits. Carefully place the shaped dough on the paper, on a baking sheet and bake in the preheated oven for 8–15 minutes depending on size. The gingerbread is cooked once it puffs up slightly and has darkened a little; don't let it get too dark at the edges. Once baked, leave the gingerbread to cool for 10 minutes on the tray before transferring to a wire rack.

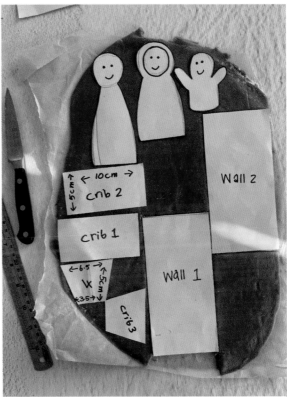

To decorate

1 Place half the instant royal icing into the bowl of a mixer. Add the water and beat slowly.
2 Once combined, add the remaining instant royal icing and more water if necessary. The icing should be thick and meringue-like but smooth enough to be piped.
3 Assemble all the sweets, icing and tools that you will need to decorate the gingerbread.
4 Start by decorating the characters. Very little icing is needed. Fit a piping bag with a small plain nozzle and fill with the icing (see page 28 for how to fill a piping bag). Carefully pipe around the outline of each character and outline any details such as the hands, beard (for Joseph) and clothes.
5 Add various sweets and edible decorations while the icing is still wet. Leave the characters to dry while you assemble the stable.
6 Position the large back wall of the stable on the cake board and use a thick line of icing to stick it in place, using drinking glasses to hold it there while the icing sets. Pipe a line of icing along one vertical edge of the back wall. Stick a side wall onto this line. I like to pipe an additional strengthening line of icing down the inside and back of the joint. Repeat with the other side wall. Next pipe icing along the tops of the walls and place the roof on. Pipe icing in between the roof joints and hold in place firmly for a minute or so while it sets.
7 Leave the icing to set for 10 minutes before continuing.
8 Pipe icing in a zigzag pattern on the roof, then stick on the sweets in rows like slates. Dot little multicoloured dragées between the sweets.
9 Pipe a cloud-shaped outline around the stable. Flood this area with icing and stick all the characters in place while it is still wet. Sprinkle liberally with glittering granulated sugar. Leave to dry.

Lilly's tips

▶ The gingerbread crib can be decorated in white icing or a mixture of colours, depending on the look you want. I've gone for a simpler white outline, but if you'd like colour, create the outlines in your coloured icing of choice and then fill them in. You can add details like Joseph's beard or headdress. Make it your own and personalise it to your own taste.

Potpourri

A medium-sized bowl
Fir or spruce trimmings from the
Christmas tree, or use rosemary
Dried pinecones and acorns
Dried orange slices (see tip)
Essential oils such as eucalyptus,
pine, orange, peppermint, clove

My elderly neighbour used to dry out all her roses and had paper bags full of them all around her house, which she'd decant into little bowls. Peggy was the first person to introduce me to the idea of potpourri. Traditionally, in seventeenth-century France, flower petals were layered with sea salt and strong spices, then stored in special vases that let the aroma drift around the room. In the 1990s it really took off: bowls of strongly perfumed wood chips and orange pieces that looked deceptively like potato crisps appeared on the backs of toilets, on coffee tables and in hallways. They were headache-inducing, drenched in overpowering manufactured scents.

But the idea of it is so lovely: dried flowers and natural scents. I think potpourri is very festive and can be done right with some tasteful pinecones, trimmings from your Christmas tree and drops of essential oils. It's divine! A bowl of this makes a lovely centrepiece on your coffee table and will gently scent the room with citrus, pine or eucalyptus. Clean, seasonal and natural.

Method

1 Arrange the tree trimmings or rosemary in the bowl. Tuck in the orange slices and top with the pinecones and acorns.
2 Add a few drops of your essential oils to the pinecones. I like to use a mix of orange and eucalyptus. Top it up with more essential oils once a week if necessary.

Lilly's tips

▶ Dry orange slices by slicing oranges into ½cm–1cm rounds and bake in your oven at its lowest setting for 2–3 hours. Place on a rack and leave them to dry out further in a warm spot, like the hot press or airing cupboard. Alternatively, dry in a dehydrator. Store in an airtight container. Ideal for festive decorating and garnishing cocktails.

Reusable Christmas crackers

What you'll need:

6 A4 pieces of felt
Embroidery thread
Embroidery needle
Sweets, jokes written on paper,
   paper hats, trinkets, etc.
Greaseproof paper
6 toilet roll tubes
Scissors
Ribbon

I love the tradition of Christmas crackers but always feel a pang of guilt. What about the environment? All those tiny plastic trinkets inside, all that paper, plastic and unnecessary packaging! We spend all year teaching our children how to reuse, repair and recycle, so it's a missed opportunity to reinforce those lessons. Making reusable crackers is so much nicer and we get to keep our own ones each year, swap them or personalise them with family names. It's a fun activity to do, writing out the cracker jokes or tucking notes inside, choosing the sweets, even making paper crowns ourselves. You can tuck almost anything into these lovely crackers. I make them with felt because they hold their shape well and involve no sewing. Keep any bright ribbons from packaging you get throughout the year – often boxes of chocolates have the nicest ones! You can glue on pretty rick-rack trimmings and do a little embroidery, or sew on a panel of patterned fabric. They really complete a table setting and can be used several times over the festive season. A box of these filled with sweets and jokes makes a really lovely gift.

Method

1 First decorate the felt. I do some simple embroidery in different patterns around the centre line of the piece, keeping in mind this will be the main body of the cracker. You can learn some simple embroidery steps on page 325.
2 Make little packages of sweets with the greaseproof paper, including any notes, trinkets or paper hats. Tuck these inside the toilet roll tube.
3 Lay the tube at one end of the felt piece and roll it up in the felt. Tie each end with a ribbon. Repeat with each piece of felt and cardboard tube.
4 Now they're ready to place on each table setting.

Lilly's tips

▶ Sanitise your toilet roll tubes by placing them on the centre of the rack in a preheated oven, 100°C, for 15 minutes to heat through and kill any bacteria. Don't leave unattended.

Orange pomander

What you'll need:

Oranges
Cloves
Toothpick
Optional: cinnamon for dusting
Ribbon or string and needle for
   hanging the finished pomander

Orange pomanders are what we make while watching Christmas films with the stove lit and a gale blowing outside. I just love this tradition. It's quite meditative pushing the cloves into the dimpled surface of the oranges. It often results in a zesty vapour that makes the whole room smell amazing. It's on my list of 'things to do in the run up to Christmas that make me feel Christmassy', along with watching all of the *Die Hard* and Indiana Jones films as well as *Pride and Prejudice* (BBC series ideally but 2005 film at least).

Medieval herbalists used pomanders to ward off illness or bring strength and good fortune. There were many different varieties but clove-studded oranges are the one that has stood the test of time. You can cover the orange completely in cloves, or just create a pattern on some of the surface. As it dries it will release a beautiful, warming spiced-citrus smell. If you want your pomanders to last, make them ahead of time and store them in a paper bag for a few weeks to dry out before use. Use lots of cloves as they are a natural preserving agent; they'll help draw out the juices as the oranges shrink in size. I like to dust mine in cinnamon to help dry them too – it's antifungal and smells so good.

Method

1 You can use a toothpick to mark out your design; this will make it easier to push in the cloves too. Or you can just randomly insert the cloves all over the orange, pressing them in firmly. The orange will shrink as it dries, so it's important you push the cloves right in tightly.

2 Once you're happy with your design you can tie the orange up with ribbon (use a needle to thread the ribbon through the orange's skin), or dust it with cinnamon to help it dry out.

3 Hang pomanders from your Christmas tree, arrange them in a bowl, stack them in a pyramid or just hang them by a source of heat so they release their lovely scent as they dry all winter long.

Chocolate Yule log

What you'll need:

6 large eggs
150g caster sugar
100g self-raising flour
40g cocoa powder

For the icing and decorating:

110g salted butter, softened
460g icing sugar, sieved
80g cocoa powder, sieved
100ml–120ml milk (or use Irish cream
    liqueur for an adults' dessert)
1 tsp vanilla extract
Optional extras: chocolate for
    making leaves and bark, marzipan
    mushrooms, rosemary, extra icing
    sugar for dusting

The Yule log was originally a pagan tradition. A large log would be specially selected, then lit in the fire on winter solstice night to symbolise the rebirth of the sun. It would be kept burning for 12 days. Burning the log would serve both spiritual and practical purposes, as it offered prosperity and warmth.

I really wanted to create a very special cake that doesn't require a trip to the shops or lots of special ingredients. So this divine Yule log cake is made from pantry staples like cocoa and flour. No cream or couverture needed here! You can whip this up at the last minute.

You can use the chocolate buttercream on its own or melt some chocolate to make the leaves and bark. Painting the backs of bay leaves makes very pretty decorations that are gorgeous on cupcakes too. I've added the traditional marzipan mushrooms and some sugar-dusted rosemary for an organic, natural, just-stepped-out-of-the-forest look. This is a very pretty cake that makes a gorgeous table centrepiece and the perfect dessert.

Method

For the cake:
1 Preheat the oven to 200°C. Line a Swiss roll tin with non-stick baking paper.
2 Whisk the eggs and sugar in the bowl of a stand mixer or with an electric whisk until pale, light and frothy.
3 Sieve the flour and cocoa powder into the bowl. Use a spatula to cut through the light egg mix, folding in the flour and cocoa as you go. Try not to beat out any air. A light touch is needed here.
4 Once combined, pour the batter into the lined tin and spread out evenly into the corners.
5 Bake for 8–10 minutes until the edges have shrunk away from the sides of the tin.
6 Place a large piece of baking paper on your worktop. Invert the cake onto the paper, and peel off the first piece of baking paper attached to the bottom of the cake. Roll the cake up tightly with the new paper inside. Leave to cool while you make the icing.

For the icing:
1 Beat the butter with half the icing sugar in a bowl until light and fluffy. Add the remaining icing sugar and the cocoa, milk and vanilla. The more you mix this, the lighter and fluffier it will become.

To assemble:
1 Uncurl the Swiss roll and remove the paper. Spread a layer of icing over the surface – you don't need too much – then re-roll tightly.
2 Next for the fun part! Cut off ¼ of the cake using a diagonal cut to make it look more natural and show a nice cross-section of the Swiss roll. Place the large part of the cake on a serving platter. Angle the cut-off piece onto the side of the cake to make it look like a branch. Use the chocolate buttercream to stick it in place.
3 Spread a layer of buttercream over the entire cake. You can use a fork to create a wood effect or cover the cake with the chocolate shards (see below).
4 Place the mushrooms and chocolate leaves (if using) in place. Tuck sprigs of rosemary around the edges. Dust the entire cake with icing sugar or a little cocoa powder.

Lilly's tips

▶ To make the shards of bark, melt 200g chocolate in a heatproof bowl over a pan of simmering water. Line a tray with greaseproof paper. Spread the chocolate onto the paper in a thin, even layer. Once the chocolate has set, you can break it into random shards that look like tree bark.
▶ To make the leaves, simply use a pastry brush to paint the backs of bay or mint leaves with melted chocolate. Leave to set fully before peeling the leaves away.

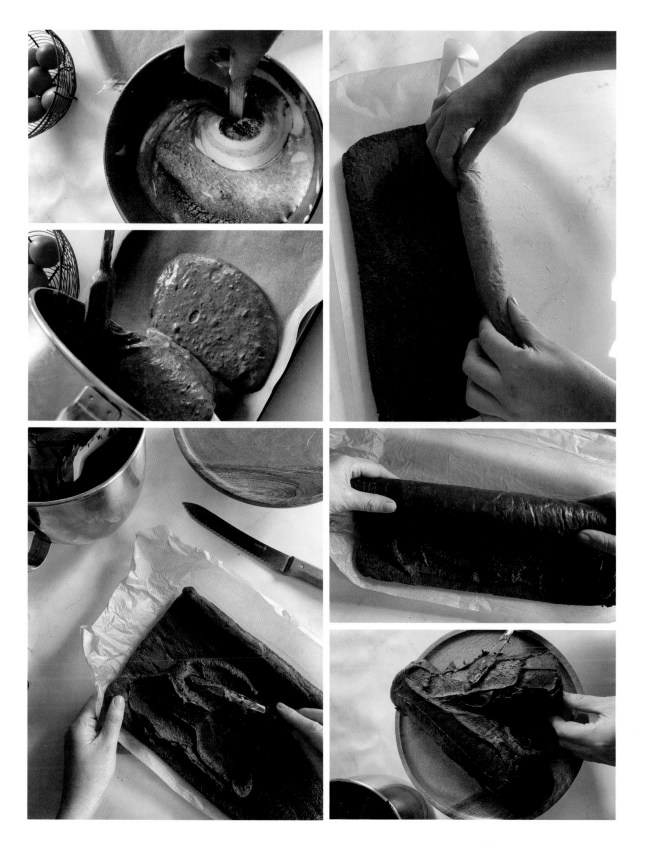

Paper snowflakes

What you'll need:

Pencil or pen
Lightweight paper
Scissors

I love that iconic scene in the movie *Elf* where the hero spends the entire night decorating the department store with paper snowflakes to welcome Santa. There's something so pure and achievable about the humble paper snowflake. Every real snowflake is different, and that's true too for these little handmade beauties. Any scraps of paper, unused colouring books or barely drawn-on sketch paper can be used. I love using gold paper from chocolate bars, brown paper bags or even newspapers to make pretty decorations. These are beautiful on a Christmas tree, with greenery on a mantelpiece or hung from a central lamp shade. Hang them in your windows with transparent thread for an elegant frosty scene, or just stick them on walls or doors in various different sizes for impact. These are one of those lovely handmade Christmas crafts that make something out of nothing. Half the fun is sitting at the kitchen table and the way everyone who comes into the room can't help but want to make one, the floor littered with tiny little flecks of snow once we're all done.

Method

1 Start with a square piece of paper, and fold it in half along the diagonal.
2 Fold it in half again to bring the two acute-angled corners together.
3 Fold this paper triangle in thirds, overlapping the left-hand pointed corner over the triangle.
4 Overlap the right-hand pointed corner over the triangle.
5 Next you can trim the pointed ends to make it a perfect triangle or leave them.
6 Now it's time to cut out the design. Draw the templates and have fun seeing how each one unfolds.
7 Unfold the snowflakes gently. Iron out any creases by pressing a sheet of paper over the snowflakes and ironing on a low setting.

Calendar

What you'll need:

Paper or card
Scissors
Glue
Pressed flowers, photos or children's drawings
Pens or markers
Hole punch
Twine or ribbon

It's the perfect time to make a calendar. There's a fresh start and so much potential in the coming year. Making your own calendar means you can fit everything you need into the pages, add a few extra pages if you have busy summer holidays or personalise it with all your family's and friends' birthdays and anniversaries. You can use photos, trinkets, kids' drawings or dried flowers to symbolise each month. Despite having the date on our watches and phones, it's still lovely to be able to have an overall view of the year ahead, a physical representation of the future and what we have planned for it. Making a calendar is part of that planning process, thinking about what we would like to do, achieve and how we would like to live in the coming year.

I think of my calendar as the perfect way to use pressed flowers. Using a flower from each month is a lovely way to enjoy the garden and remind myself what will be coming into bloom soon. Children's drawings or photos are also ideal.

January

S	M	T	W	T	F	S
						1
2	3	4	5	6	7	
8	9	10	11	12	13	14
15	16	17	(18)	19	20	21
22	23	24	25	26	27	28
29	30	31				

18th Cathals' Birthday.

Method

1 Trim all the sheets of paper or cardboard to the same size. I like to halve A4-sized sheets of card lengthways. It's a handy shape for hanging.
2 Choose a flower or image to correspond to each month.
3 If using flowers, roll the glue onto the paper first, then press the delicate flower in place.
4 Glue each flower, photo or drawing to the top ⅓ of each rectangle.
5 Write the months, days and dates below.
6 Personalise the calendar with birthdays and special days.
7 Add a section for notes at the end.
8 Use a hole punch to make a hole in the top of each page.
9 String the pages together with twine or ribbon and hang the calendar where you can see it.

Junk journal for Nollaig na mBan

What you'll need:

Scrapbook paper, tea-dyed papers (see tip below), wrapping paper, homemade paper, old book or magazine pages

Cardboard or cereal box card for the cover

Scissors

Glue

Bulldog clips to hold the paper in place

Needle

Embroidery thread

Nollaig na mBan, or Women's Christmas, falls on 6 January and it is traditional for the men to cook and the women to rest, as they would have done all of the work over the festive season. It's the twelfth and final day of Christmas, and it's usually when the last of the Christmas decorations are taken down. Nowadays it's a day for mothers, daughters, aunts and female friends to just get together after the busy festive season. I think it's the perfect opportunity for a crafternoon. I always build up such a collection of paper over Christmas – brown paper, magazines, cards and wrappers. Get your best buddies together with a bottle of something nice, chat and make a lovely junk journal with your paper stash.

A junk journal is a bound book created with scrap paper and things that otherwise might end up in landfill. It's a great way to avoid paper waste. You can create beautiful pages and incorporate things like fabric, receipts and photos that mean something to you. Add to it throughout the year and you can admire a fully complete junk journal this time next year!

Method

1 Fold all your pages in half. Tear the pages to size, measuring them by eye as you go. The more organic and relaxed the style is, the better. Cut any pages that don't suit being torn. Compile them into signatures: collections of 4 folded sheets. Sit the pages of each signature all into one another. Make 10 of these signatures.

2 Measure the card to make the cover; it should be slightly larger than the signatures. Glue an extra strip of card or paper to the spine to make it stronger.

3 Find the centre page of each signature. Make sure the pages are all evenly placed and lined up. Clip one side with the bulldog clip. Mark where you want to place 3 holes evenly down the centre crease of the pages – one in the centre and one either side. Then poke holes with the needle. Poke corresponding holes in the spine.

4 Thread the needle through the middle hole in the first signature, then place the signature into the cover and thread through. Thread through the holes either side, and finally thread through the middle hole again and tie the thread ends together tightly. The signature is now sewn into the cover. Repeat with the remaining signatures.

Lilly's tips

▶ Dye your paper by spattering it with strong tea, or paint over the pages with a thick brush. Leave to dry, then iron with a piece of fabric over it or flatten by placing a heavy book on top.

▶ Add little pockets and sleeves in which to stash photos or mementos.

▶ Look in charity shops for old books that have interesting pages that you can use.

Yoga mat cleaner spray

What you'll need:

1 × 450ml spray bottle
250ml water
125ml witch hazel
10 drops lavender essential oil
10 drops lemon essential oil
5 drops peppermint essential oil
3 drops tea tree essential oil

There's nothing worse than trying to maintain a plank and noticing your mat is not the freshest! I try to do all I can to make myself more likely to do a little bit of yoga or Pilates each day. I love running but I find Pilates has just the right mix of mindfulness, stretching and workout that I need. Reformer Pilates is on another level, the absolute best – if you haven't tried it then give it a go! It's so much fun too. At home, though, I like to do yoga or Pilates through guided YouTube videos. It's a great way to keep practising when you can't make it to a class.

To use this lovely mixture, just spray directly onto your yoga mat. A light, even coating is ideal. Use a clean towel to rub the spray into your mat and wipe away any excess. Leave to dry completely before rolling up or using.

I chose this combination of oils because it smells amazing and has natural antibacterial properties too. Double win! Not only will this spray ensure you have a squeaky clean workout, it'll also ensure that with each deep breath you're inhaling clean, stimulating smells that make it even more Zen.

Alternative blends

Cleaning and deodorising: 10 drops peppermint and 10 drops patchouli

Relaxing: 10 drops lavender and 10 drops bergamot

Method

1 Pour the water and witch hazel into the bottle.
2 Add the essential oils.
3 Shake and spray directly onto the mat.
4 Wipe clean using a towel and leave to dry completely.
5 Use after each session.
6 If you prefer a stronger smell, add more oils, or more of the one you love most.

Paper-making

What you'll need:

2 wooden photo frames with glass
removed; I used A5 size
1 rectangle of net fabric, fine mesh
or gauze (for example old net
curtains)
Staple gun
Old paper (drawings, discarded
sheets, junk mail, brown paper,
envelopes, etc.)
1 wide rectangular tub (I use one
of the kids' toy buckets, but a
washing-up basin is also ideal)
Stick blender
Towels
Scrap pieces of fabric, roughly A4
size – undyed or colourfast, to
avoid staining the paper
Absorbent sponge

Can I just say I'm obsessed with paper-making and will spend my retirement years focusing solely on this? It's so massively rewarding to transform old scraps of paper or toilet paper rolls into something so beautiful and delicate. I made paper years ago in college and really loved the process. I wanted to make this a project that you can actually do in your own home without investing in any special equipment, so I'm including directions here for how to make your own mould and deckle. You can buy these ready-made too, of course. Before long you can be making your own headed paper, cards, and even books with these beautiful sheets.

Take the process one step further and make your own calendar or journal (see page 300 or 305). The texture and look of the papers are something really special and will make any project look unique.

Method

1 If you're making your own mould and deckle, begin by stretching the mesh or net over one of the frames. Staple it in place. This will need to be very taut, so stretch the fabric and ensure it's tightly wrapped around the frame. This mesh-covered frame is now your mould. The other frame is the deckle that will sit on top and ensure that your pages have straight edges.

2 Next, tear the paper into tiny pieces. A paper shredder is very handy here! I do find tearing it up is easy, though, and kids love to help with this step. Place the torn paper into the large basin and fill about halfway with water. Leave it to soak for 12 hours. Soaking it for this length of time will break down the fibres.

3 Use a stick blender to blitz the paper into a fine pulp. The finer the pulp, the smoother the paper.

4 You can then add a little more water if the pulp is too thick. Judge it by eye: the paper pulp should just coat your hand when you take out a scoop. It should be like a thick smoothie.

5 Stack your mould and deckle by placing the mould screen-side up and laying the deckle upside down on top. Hold them tightly together.

6 Next slide your mould and deckle vertically into the water. Keep the two together. Shimmy them to even out the paper pulp as it rests inside the mould. If it's too thick, your paper will be too, so just a light layer is enough. Lift the mould and deckle out of the basin. Tap out as much water as possible. Remove the top empty frame (the deckle) by pulling it straight up.

7 Lay a folded towel on your work surface and place a piece of fabric on top.

8 Turn your mould over onto the fabric, with the paper pulp facing down. Use a sponge to press down on the back of the mesh and remove as much water as you can. Lift the mould straight up and there's your sheet of paper on the fabric!

9 Leave the fabric with the wet paper attached to dry; either lay it flat or or hang it up. Once the fabric and paper are completely dry, you can easily peel the paper off.

Kombucha

What you'll need:

200g organic sugar

15g green tea leaves (loose-leaf or teabags are ideal; matcha powder is not suitable)

500ml–1 litre kombucha (shop-bought or from a homemade batch)

1 kombucha scoby

A very large bowl

Sieve

A container for brewing the kombucha, such as a very large jar or drinks dispenser

A muslin or other cotton cloth

Elastic band

Makes 3–4 litres

Committing to improving your gut microbiome is a really great new year's resolution. Your microbes affect your immune system, your digestion and mood. The more varied our diet is the better, so including lots of prebiotic and probiotic food is ideal. Kombucha is a very ancient fermented tea drink that's slightly effervescent. The culture that works its magic on the sweetened tea is called a scoby: a symbiotic culture of bacteria and yeast. Together the bacteria and yeast convert the sugar to alcohol (it's a byproduct, and usually kombucha contains about 0.5 per cent alcohol). This creates a delicious fizzy, tangy drink that can be flavoured in so many ways. The best part is that it's easy to make and you can even make your own scoby. All you need is time. Or get a scoby from your local kombucha (booch) maker – you could also buy one online from a reputable fermenter.

During the summer we love to have the fridge stocked up with our own kombucha. You can give it a second ferment with berries or fruit to flavour it and make it even more carbonated. The possibilities are endless. It's a fantastic fizzy option to have at hand on hot summer days, so get brewing now and your kombucha stores will be well established in a few months.

I make continuous-brew kombucha in a Kilner drinks dispenser. That way there's no need to disturb the scoby with each batch. Just drain out what you need and top it up with sweetened tea as per the directions below.

Growing your own scoby

Buy two bottles of unpasteurised raw kombucha. There are plenty of really great Irish brands to choose from. I like to buy two different ones to vary the bacteria and yeasts. Pour both bottles into a large wide-mouthed jar. Don't put the lid on; instead use a piece of muslin or other cloth and fasten over the top of the jar with an elastic band to let it breathe. Within a few days you'll notice a cloudy film begin to appear – that's your scoby! Like magic. This floating jelly is also known as a mother. Once two weeks have passed the scoby will be thick enough to begin your kombucha-making journey!

Method

1 Place the sugar in a very large, wide bowl. Add 500ml boiling water, then stir to dissolve.
2 Top up this sweetened water with 2–3 litres of cooled boiled water.
3 Add the green tea and stir well. Leave to brew for 15 minutes.
4 Pour the sweet tea through a sieve and into your brewing container. I use a large Kilner with a tap dispenser, which is very handy for bottling.
5 Add 500ml–1 litre of kombucha, either bought or from a previous batch.
6 Add the precious scoby and tightly cover the top of the container with a cloth, securing with an elastic band.
7 Leave at room temperature for at least one week, then taste it and see if it tastes good to you. It should have a nice balance of acidity and sweetness. If you want more acidity, brew it for a few days longer. Bottle it or flavour it when it's still slightly sweet so that it will continue to ferment and get fizzier.
8 You can now bottle it and store in the fridge, or flavour the booch by doing a second ferment (see below).

Lilly's tips

▶ To do a second ferment you can top up the bottled kombucha with fruit juice, or add fruit such as raspberries, or pineapple and chillies, to the bottle and strain out after a few days. The sugar in the fruit will further ferment the drink, making it fizzier and giving it a gorgeous flavour.

Knitted kitchen dishcloth

What you'll need:

1 × 50g ball of cotton yarn suitable
   for 4.5mm needles
4.5mm needles
Darning needle
Scissors

This is a very easy and rewarding craft as it only requires basic knitting skills – you can find my guide to introductory knitting techniques on page 326. The little knitted scrubbers are very handy as pot stands, as scourers or instead of paper towels. The garter stitch provides a nice texture for cleaning.

A simple garter-stitch single-colour dishcloth is one of the easiest things to knit. When I was little, I used to constantly knit squares as dolls' blankets and sewed them all together to make a patchwork. Having to knit a simple square is a good way to perfect your knitting and concentrate on getting your garter stitch right. This project is very portable too, so perfect for keeping in your bag or car for whenever you get a chance to knit a few rows. You can also change the colours and do stripes of varying thickness. Match them to your kitchen! A stack of these handknit cloths in various colours makes a lovely housewarming gift with a nice soap or eco-friendly dishwashing liquid.

Method

1 Cast on 48 stitches.
2 Row 1: knit to the end of the row.
3 Continue to knit every row until the piece measures 25cm.
4 Cast off.
5 Weave in the ends of the yarn using the darning needle.

Lilly's guide to sewing and embroidery

I love to sew, and you don't need much to get started with simple handsewn crafts: just a needle and thread and whatever material you'd like to use. Pins are also helpful to hold your fabric together until the stitches are in place! Here are four basic stitches that you can use to complete the projects in this book.

Running stitch

1. This straight stitch is the most basic sewing stitch, in which you pass your needle in and out through the material at regular intervals. Bring your needle up at point 1, and then insert it down a stitch length away at point 2. Bring it up again at point 3 and repeat along the line, keeping your stitches as even as possible.

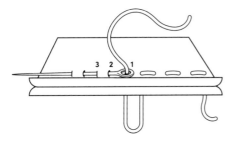

Satin stitch

1. This stitch can be used to fill in small areas. Pull your needle through to the front of your fabric at point 1. Make single, straight stitches, inserting the needle at point 2 and out again at point 3. Keep your stitches as close together as possible, so that the area fills smoothly with no gaps.

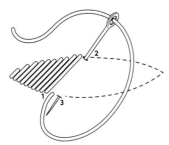

Slip stitch

1. Also known as a ladder stitch, this stitch is perfect for closing seams or bringing edges together. Bring your needle up at point 1, and then down through the fabric on the opposite edge at point 2. Come up again on the same side at point 3, a stitch length away. Repeat this technique to bring the two pieces of material together, going back and forth on each side of the seam.

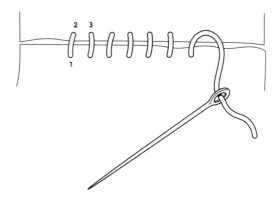

Whip stitch

1. This stitch can be used to join two pieces of fabric together. Align your material so that one edge matches, and then start and the right side and move left. Insert your needle through both pieces of fabric at point 1, and then bring it over the top and round the back to insert again at point 2.

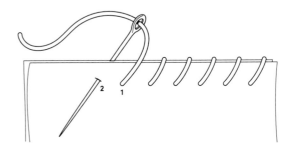

Embroidery is one of my favourite crafts, as it can make even the simplest project look beautiful and unique. As for sewing, you'll be using a needle and thread, but with embroidery the focus is on embellishment rather than structure. Here are four of my favourite embroidery stitches.

Cross stitch

1. You may have seen cross stitching before; it's one of the simplest and most popular embroidery stitches. First, bring your needle and thread through the fabric from point 1 to point 2 (and repeat) to sew a row of evenly spaced diagonal lines. When you've sewed the length you want, stitch diagonally back over the first row to create crosses. Try to use the same holes if you can, to keep things neat.

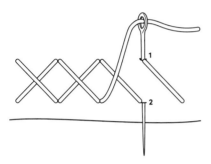

Back stitch

1. This stitch can often be used to create outlines, as the stitches are usually run together to create a solid line. Bring your needle up through the fabric at point 1, a stitch-length away from the point where you want your pattern to start. Then bring it back down at point 2 to make a simple stitch from right to left. Continue by bringing the needle up another stitch-length to the right of point 1, and repeat.

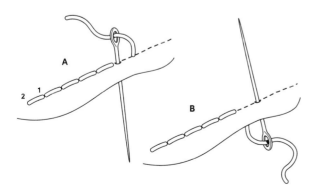

Blanket stitch

1. This technique can provide a pretty decorative finish along the edges of a project. Pull your needle through to the front of your material at point 1. Then push it through to the back at point 2 and come up again at point 3, making sure to hold the thread under the needle as you pull the stitch tight.

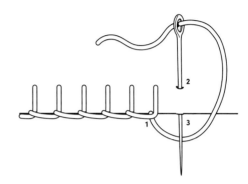

French knot

1. French knots are useful for creating texture in your embroidery via a raised point – this could be the centre of a flower, for example. Pull your needle up through your fabric to the front at point 1. Then, holding your thread taut, wrap it twice around your needle, staying close to the material. Insert your needle back through the fabric at point 2; this should be as close as possible to point 1 without going into the same hole. Keep the thread taut as you sew through, and pull until you have a raised knot.

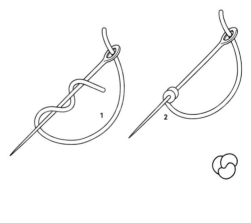

Lilly's guide to knitting

Knitting is slightly more complicated than sewing, but once you know the basics, the range of crafts you'll be able to undertake is amazing! Here are four simple stitches to start you off. You'll need needles and cotton yarn – I recommend using fairly chunky yarn and needles to begin with, just because they're easier to grip. Try using wood or bamboo needles for the same reason. Use a darning needle once you've cast off to tidy up your knitting.

Casting on

1. First up, this is how you get the yarn onto your needles. Drape the loose end of the yarn over your left thumb and the ball end (this is known as the working yarn) over your left index finger. Use your other fingers to hold yarn lengths against your left palm, and insert one needle upward through the loop on your thumb.

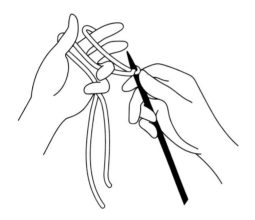

2. Using the needle, catch the working yarn from your index finger and pull it through the loop on your thumb. Remove your thumb from the loop. Still holding the ends of the yarn in your palm, reposition your thumb and tighten a new stitch on the right-hand needle. Repeat until you've cast on the number of stitches that you want.

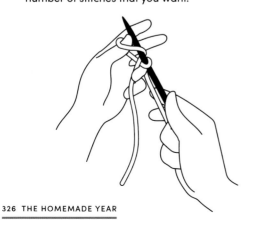

Garter stitch

1. Also known as a knit stitch, this is the main technique you'll use to actually *knit*. Hold the needle with cast-on stitches in your left hand. Wrap the working yarn around your left index finger and hold it behind the left needle. Insert your right needle into your first cast-on stitch on the left needle, opening up a stitch.

2. Catch the working yarn with your right needle and pull it through the opened stitch. Slip the first cast-on stitch off the left needle, while holding the second stitch so that it doesn't slip off as well. The stitch on the right needle is your first garter stitch! Continue along your cast-on row until you have completed it, and then swap your needles over, so that the one with the stitches is once again in your left hand.

Purl stitch

1. A purl stitch is the opposite of a garter stitch in two ways: the working yarn is held in front of your project rather than behind it, and the needle is inserted from the back to the front instead of the other way round. So: wrap your working yarn around your left index finger, hold it in front of your knitting and insert the right needle – from back to front – into the first cast-on stitch.

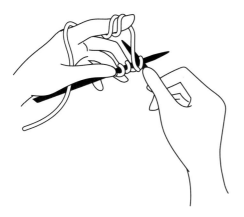

2. Then move your left index finger down so that the working yarn is laid over the needle from front to back. Push the working yarn through the cast-on stitch. Slip the first cast-on stitch off your left needle, ensuring that no other stitches slip off. Now your first purl stitch is on the right needle. Carry on until the end of the row, and then swap your needles over.

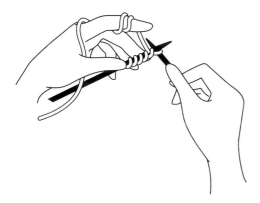

Casting off

1. Now let's look at how to get the yarn off your needles. Casting off stops your stitches from unravelling once the needles are no longer holding them in place. Knit two (garter) stitches and insert your left needle into the first stitch. Lift this stitch over the second stitch and off the needle.

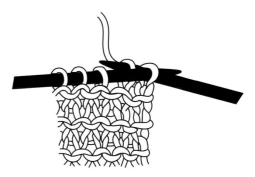

2. Continue knitting stitches like this until all stitches have been cast off. Cut the working yarn, leaving a tail that's about 15cm long, or approximately the length of your hand. Pull this tail through the last stitch to secure.

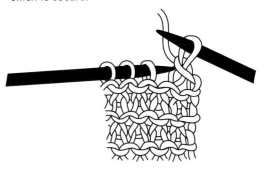

3. Use a darning needle to weave the tail ends of your yarn through the back of several stitches, to make sure everything looks lovely and tidy.

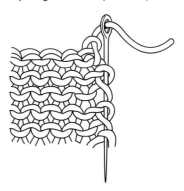

Lilly's list of suppliers

Cork Art Supplies
www.corkartsupplies.com
For all art supplies, including paints, clay, spray paint, brushes and more.

Vibes and Scribes
www.vibesandscribes.ie
For art supplies, wool, felt and fabric.

Riot Rye
www.riotrye.ie
Detailed recipes and tutorials for sourdough breadmaking, as well as a bake shop for buying fantastic organic flours, ready-made sourdough starter and baking equipment such as tins and lames (for scoring dough).

This is Knit
www.thisisknit.ie
All the tools, accessories and wool you'll need to knit.

Ground Wellbeing
www.groundwellbeing.com
Natural, sustainable essential oil blends created in Ireland.

Kotanical
www.kotanical.ie
Irish essential oils company sourcing locally and ethically.

NeighbourFood
www.neighbourfood.ie
I find NeighbourFood so amazing. It's an online market connecting local farmers and producers to customers. Check and see if there's one in your area! It's where I get free-range meat, organic vegetables and fruit, speciality flours and bulk apple cider vinegar.

All About Kombucha
www.allaboutkombucha.ie
An Irish-made organic kombucha brewery that sells scobies, teas and everything you need to get started brewing your own kombucha.

River Run Ferments
www.riverrunferments.com
For all things fermentation see the brilliant Terri Ann Fox's website and follow her on Instagram (@river_run_ferments). She runs workshops and sells scobies and sourdough starter.